Finding a Place to Park my Melon

Katherine Gostick

Copyright © 2020 Katherine Gostick

ISBN: 9798688543599

DEDICATION

To all the fruits in my basket, but most of all my loyal travel companions, Dominic, James, Edward, Henry and Matilda who bring me joy, laughter and acceptance, and my mother Veronica Croasdale who instilled in me the resilience I needed to make it through my adventures and acts as my proof reader and editor.

CONTENTS

OTHER BOOKS BY KATE GOSTICK

The Spy who Saved Christmas

Coming soon
Your Haemorrhoids are not my Fault!

PREFACE

Travel is said to widen your horizons and, for me, it brought with it no regrets. My failures brought with them on the whole, a funny story and scope for growth and my successes brought a feeling of accomplishment and a knowledge that it is always worth giving things a try.

Travel definitely made me more aware of differences, both those I chose to embrace and those I chose to reject. This is a story of my experiences of living between three cultures, never quite knowing how or where to fit in.

My views of those cultures may not match those of the reader, but that's ok and I offer no apology.

My spelling may not match that of the reader, maybe because they speak a different form of English or maybe just because I am a terrible proof reader. I offer no apologies for that either, but request forgiveness for the latter!

The recollections of event are mine and may not match those of others. The names of the people involved, may differ slightly from those of the real characters, whose lives you will delve into, but I feel I owe them a little privacy. After all their exploits gave me the funny stories I have to tell you. Again I offer no apology

So, take my hand, and let's take a journey together. No regrets, no apologies. Just enjoy the ride!

Finding a Place to Park my Melon

1 FINDING A PLACE TO PARK MY MELON

"I am a peach. You are a melon. They are Coconuts." This, in short, was our cultural training from an American, to two Brits telling us how to try and assimilate into German culture. The peach will open up to you, allowing you to penetrate towards the heart which burns within them, but you will hit the stone and never be allowed to access the real person at that heart. We were melons. You only had to sit next to us for five minutes on a bus and that would be long enough to penetrate the surface and allow the contents to gush out all over you. The German coconuts, waiting for us across the Atlantic, would need a sledgehammer to penetrate the solid outer coating, but once you were in you were in, the hard shell would remain broken revealing the contents in its full glory.

I was not only born a melon in a field of melons, but came from the field where the melons, from which I was propagated, had grown since the 12th century when surnames came to be and grounded us in the set of rules we must adhere to. However, I longed to be part of an assorted tropical fruit basket. This has always made me 'the other' even when my DNA professed that I was firmly rooted in that field, when the tiny circle that suggested the source of my ancestry, was dropped where I was born. My story is all about being 'the other.' At first, finding my own permission to inhabit 'the other' where I feel secure and then accepting that, for my mother, 'the other' is a place of danger I needed to be protected from.

In Malaysia, we truly were 'the other'. It was a land of tiny, tiny, teeny weeny, little people with darker skin, black hair and deep, dark, black eyes who spoke a different language, worshipped different deities, and ate the durian fruit that smelled of death. Into this land we arrived, giants with hair like fire and gold, skin like snow, eyes like ice, melons to the core. We were truly 'other'. We chose to go to the places where people like us did not go, where nobody uttered our words or worshipped our God. As we wandered along the streets where wives shook husbands' arms alerting them to the invasion, and cell phones surreptitiously snapped our photos recording the aliens that had landed from, who knows where. This was a whole new level of 'other,' I thought, as I chose a hijab off the rack and pulled the long, blue, loose-fitting garments over my head and over the heads of my sons. I reached up to put one over the ginger curls that had created so much intrigue and sat atop Edward's six feet five inch frame, towering above the carpet which lead us into the Malacca mosque. We were the other, the extreme other yet, as women giggled around us amused by the amazonian creature with blond curls escaping the edge of her azure blue hijab, they did not fear us or resent us, instead, they were fascinated by us. We intrigued them and they welcomed us with open arms asking for selfies, their crimson lipstick smiles beaming under the frames of designer sunglasses, which were themselves framed by the traditional hijab. Our driver explained they had never seen westerners before and definitely not as extreme as a 6 ft 5" ginger. Everyone wanted to record the event. They made us feel special, welcome, wanted and interesting.

Later, Edward decided to try the Durian fruit and a crowd surrounded us, whispering amongst themselves, the giggles now heightened with anticipation. As the fruit was split open with a machete the stench filled the air, the tension grew. Would he or wouldn't he? As he wholeheartedly bit into the corpselike flesh cheers erupted in celebration of the fusing of the melon with the Durian. The differences were entertaining, invigorating, welcome, and refreshing, 'other' bound us together. Our love and respect for our differences, for life itself and its diversity, made us the same and for the first time in my life, I felt less 'other' than ever before. The following day at the water park, as I watched the people zip-lining from the cliff over the pool then splashing into the cool waters, the first wearing a full swim burka, the next a thong bikini and the next, a portly gentleman screaming in his navy swim trunks, I could not help but wonder if the same welcome and acceptance were likely to be afforded to them if they visited America or Britain.

When we lived in Germany, in Edward's class everyone was 'other.' There were twelve kids in his class, each born in a different country each sharing their religion with, at most, only two others. Everyone was 'other' so 'other' became kindred, the norm. They celebrated each other's cultures and festivals, they laughed together, cried together, learnt together, and then returned home to their own language, traditions, and religion richer for what they had shared. Being 'the other' is a gift tainted only by those who reject 'other' rather than embracing it.

In Germany, I was a melon squashed at the bottom of the plastic crate of coconuts. My ability to sit neatly nestled in amongst the dark, hairy fruit, bringing a little sweetness, so I thought, to the milky liquid and hard unyielding flesh was resented in some, but not by all. Only

3

coconuts were acceptable in some crates. Far from bringing sweetness, I added a note of bitterness to the most bitter crates of fruit despite my best efforts.

As I sat in the American hairdressers, a melon in a room full of peaches, before me was a line of identical women, each with identical haircuts, bleach blonde, identical black, NorthFace jackets hanging on the pegs by the door, all in a line. Outside identical oversized cars sat in a line, identical to that of their owners waiting to transport identical children to identical sports which changed uniformly with each season. They spoke, but said nothing, then blown dry into uniformity, they each drove home to their identical husbands to discuss how we should limit the arrival of 'other' with a wall. "Oh no! Not my other, the other other." My other was apparently fine, but I identified as the other, the one on the other side of the wall. I did not identify as a peach. Please, God, I thought, give me 'other' if this is the alternative. Let me be the passion fruit in an assorted celebration fruit basket, not the melon squashed in a crate of peaches.

Not all those who inhabited my new land were identical some were amazing fruits full of colour and variety. This is the story of the search to find my inner passion fruit, to discover those other fruits my flavours complemented and whose basket I wanted to inhabit. It is the story of how I identified those which constrained and stifled me and belonged in a heavy-duty crate of their own, far far away from my handwoven wicker basket of exotic, fun delicacies.

2 THE BIG MOVE AGAIN!

You only ever regret the things you don't do. As Edward told me, in a wisdom far beyond his years, mistakes and failures are just the great stories that make you interesting to others. When Dominic came home one day and mentioned he had been headhunted for a job in Boston Massachusetts, Edward was only a year old so had not shared his philosophies on life with me yet, but I knew somehow that this was a chance not to be missed. Dominic had never expected me to agree to move halfway across the world on a whim, leaving behind the career I had worked so hard to become successful at, to be labeled as a trailing spouse, but it would only be for two to five years until the kids started school and we would come back home for me to continue on as an optometrist. I surprised him by accepting the challenge. Nobody told me that once you move to the outside you will always be the outsider and there would never be the opportunity to go back.

Ten years later, we were still in Massachusetts and once again life had become a repetitive, drudgery, with each day blending into the next. Once again I was packing up boxes and about to embark on an adventure to make mistakes, have catastrophic failures and make life fun and interesting again. I felt uncomfortable when I made mistakes when I was the outsider who did not know the rules, but as soon as I learnt the unwritten codes things became boring and I longed for the unexpected nature of being the outsider again. So here I was watching strangers wrap every personal item I owned in bubble wrap, hoping there was not a stray piece of poorly chosen underwear that had fallen down the back of a drawer to be discovered by a hairy removal man, now privy to secrets that had only previously been shared with my husband. I divided possessions into crates for storage and for Germany, trying to figure out what we could not live without for the next two years and what was only frippery that could sit in a warehouse in Medway. I also knew that once again I must assess which parts of myself were fripperies and which the parts I could not exist without and needed to hang on to.

James like me needed security. It had been hard for him to find out, only the day before we had our first trip to Germany, that he was to leave the familiar, but Edward was excited by new adventures and longed for the unknown. The simple fact that one of the schools had a vegetarian choice on the menu every day was enough for Edward to grasp the positive and run with it. Henry didn't really understand, but said that he was excited because he knew that he would get a balloon on the plane. When we boarded the plane to Germany at 4.30 that afternoon he didn't seem to notice the absence of balloons as Edward tried to speak German and said "Guten Tag" to everyone he met. The German air hostess, unaware of the huge upheaval his little life was about to experience, told him that if she spoke to him in English he should reply in English and even if she had of known I doubt she would have cared. To our great relief, for once, we arrived devoid of vomit as Edward managed to get through the whole flight without throwing up once, following forty dollars well spent on an acupuncturist and an extra few dollars on a bottle of peppermint oil. Dominic's navigation system, which had been set to the accent of a Lincolnshire farmer, shouted out to turn left and right and was accompanied by roars of laughter from Henry who thought it was the funniest thing he had ever heard. Soon it was added by more guffawing as the boys noticed German exit signs which read "ausfahrt".

Edward's attempts to fit in right from the start involved him copying the country bumpkin accent on the sat nav which, since we were in Germany, he assumed was how he needed to now speak. A lady called Gabi who showed us around and took us to schools and houses was very understanding and tried to teach him a few German words until the Lincolnshire farmer was replaced by Dinglish, a mixture of German and English, indecipherable to either race which was probably for the best.

Gabi began with a couple of houses, to the north of Frankfurt, which were very small and surrounded by other houses. One had a very enthusiastic letting agent with extremely floppy hair who was very keen to tell us that daylight and a kitchen were included in the price. As he bounded from window to window extolling the virtues of solar rays, I had to leave the room as I fought to contain my sniggers.

The next house was close to the centre of Frankfurt, next to the racecourse. It was a big old house reminiscent of a French chateau. Parts of it were broken and needed attention, but it was full of daylight, I was assuming at no extra charge and it had character. It reminded Dominic of his Gran's house in that the different time periods the house had lived through all blended together in an eclectic mix of builtin cupboards, free standing kitchen dressers and different shaped windows all finished off with a beautiful garden of plants melting into one another in curved borders around meandering lawns. The boys hated it. It just did not feel like home to them. There was something a little creepy and as we wandered downstairs and stood next to the door of an accountant's office, which took up the whole of that lower area, Edward found a tiny little door under the stairs that was locked tight. This seemed strange since our upper floor had no lock leaving it open, through the day, to the possibility of a wandering accountant or one of his clients.

"Where does this go?" Edward inquired, curious as ever. This was the question that should never be asked. A look of panic came over the estate agent's face.

"She lives down there," he said sheepishly "But you will never see her" This I think was meant to reassure us. It turned out that not only did the house look like Dominic's Gran's, but it even had its very own grandmother living in the basement who could wander upstairs into our house at any time! Both the house with the free daylight and the one with the free grandmother were discounted.

Eventually, after more searching, we decided on a house and a school and learnt that Germans like to be naked and that Edward's lack of a filter meant German Army scouts may not be the troop for us. As we left Germany we still had no signed contract for the house, but Gabi said she would send it on and everything seemed a little more secure. We arrived back in Boston a few days later to discover that security can be short lived. The man had rented the house to somebody else so we had no house, but we kept in touch with Gabi and Dominic found a new house, close to the old town of Dreieichenhain, on a trip back for work.

As the moving day grew closer and adverts on Craig's list for the little tikes jungle climber were responded to by women sending naked pictures of themselves, legs widely spread, revealing their inner workings, unwittingly projected on to the main TV from my iPad, the rollercoaster of uncertainty that accompanies a move began. Although, a little shocking in response to an advertisement for a child's climbing frame, it could have been viewed as a tool to tease us into the more liberal German attitudes we were about to be thrust into.

As May drew to an end, the heat started to build and the trees burst into life. With only four days until we became homeless, we did what any sensible family in our predicament would do and set off to a three day rugby tournament in New Hampshire, fingers tightly crossed that we wouldn't break anyone while we were there. A few days later the house was packed up and any embarrassing items wrapped in tissue paper. The bunny became an international jet setter and set off to Germany to live with a racist bunny sitter next to the Dreieich swimming pool. We all moved into the Marriott Residence Inn to finish the school year, signed a new tenant for the house then two days before they were due to move in, for some unknown reason, we decided to have fourteen kids for a sleepover in the empty house. Henry needed a sense of belonging or a good hiding, but in his great wisdom decided to monogram the whole house in Sharpie with an "H" on every surface. Luckily we discovered that Mr. Muscle sponges remove Sharpie H's. All I had was a couple of boxes some "funking up your mutt pet shampoo" and a hand towel to have a shower, but most of all I had friends who knew Mr. Muscle sponges removed Sharpie Hs, who were a shoulder to cry on, made me tea and cake, generally fed me and even took Squishy the Japanese fighting fish, who was looking for a new home.

It was the middle of July and I felt a little bit vulnerable. I had no car, no house, three kids and a husband who had transferred all the money out of our joint accounts and into an account in just his name in Germany! Moving day arrived and Matilda was placed in a van and taken to the airport. Later that day Dominic greeted his trailing spouse with his trailing kids and later his trailing dog and welcomed us into an empty house carrying my boxes of essentials. By essentials, you may assume I mean something to eat off or drink from or maybe a pillow or blanket to lay our weary heads on in a house devoid of any furniture. I was a trailing spouse who had trailed before. I understood valued items. They weren't cups or plates or bedding, all of which could be replaced by a quick trip to Ikea. Essentials were scrapbooks and photos, jewellery and teddy bears, the items that can never be replaced that hold the keys to memories that can never be taken away.

Our neighbours, some of whom were related to our landlord, brought us mattresses when they found out we intended to spend our first couple of nights on the hard, wooden floors. They introduced us to their friends which allowed me a precious few minutes of someone else's internet since it would take a couple of weeks before we got our own.

Germans were on the whole so nice and made us feel welcome and were not what I was expecting from a shy of coconuts. We seemed to spend all our time explaining that we weren't American, which seems to please them. The container driver bringing our furniture was not as impressed as he tutted and declared my husband to be "catastrophe" since he spoke even less German than me! The first few weeks were tough trying to sort everything out without internet or a full grasp of the language. I felt like I should have been awarded the Olympic medal for the Ikea heptathlon as I managed to solve two storage problems, a seating problem, a 'we've lost the screws' problem and a lack of a grill pan problem in 42 minutes from entering the store to having a fully loaded car and leaving the car park. After gaining a new world record for the fastest Ikea visit ever my fellow male athlete was left smiling for the first time ever in this gruelling event!

If the practical aspects were not easy then the emotional part of fitting in was even harder. I just wanted to blend in and not feel like a travelling circus all the time. Henry started replying 'Ja' to everything instead of yes so he looked like a German kid with very good English, instead of an English kid with very bad German, which helped a little with the blending. James pointed out that it was hard enough to know what any girl was thinking, but when they only ever speak German, it's impossible As someone who loved math and science it was great to see my boys start to develop a love of these subjects too. James told me that for the first time he enjoyed a math class, and that I was right when I said European maths was more fun. He loved the freedom to just go and explore on your own and the education system which encouraged critical thinking rather than regurgitating facts, like in the American schools.

At first, James had been placed in a class with all German speakers, a melon peach hybrid squashed at the bottom of a crate of coconuts, which was hard for him both linguistically and culturally, but then again the language and culture brought challenges for us all. Over the next three years, our eyes would be opened to differences in language, festivals, attitudes to sex, the human body and education and a whole host of different parts of life. We would grow stronger for it and learn a lot about who we would choose to join us on our journey. This understanding makes you stronger, but also makes you 'other' as it is a precious gift only given to those, like us, who look in from outside not to those sitting comfortably within the security of the known.

3 DAS GEHT NICHT!

Language binds us together, but also identifies us as from one tribe or another. In my village growing up, a bread roll was a teacake, but in the adjoining village, it was an oven bottom or a barm cake. When it crossed over the bleak moorland of the Pennines and took its place in a Sheffield baker's window it became a bread cake, but if it was bought by a Midlander, the same piece of bread would sit on his tea table to become a cob. Your word for a bread roll, your language, defines your history, your roots. It is important because it allows you to belong or to be alien. It decides the level of acceptance you will receive and therefore creates your sense of security.

When we found out we were moving to Germany, keen to avoid not being able to communicate effectively and the terrifying consequences that may bring, I purchased Rosetta stone, but it tended to teach you bizarre stuff first like "my podiatrist is from Kathmandu". It came with an expectation that you would naturally absorb any grammar by osmosis which was flawed in its reasoning. Instead, I found myself saying "Ich bin heist" rather than "Mir ist heist" as I informed the PTO meeting that basically I was "orgasming right now" rather than, "Is it a little warm in here?", suggesting we may need to turn on the fan. In America, such a mistake would have been accompanied by shocked faces, but not questioned. A week or two later I would notice that invitations to PTO meetings would not be dropping into my inbox anymore. I would have to think back to expressions on faces from the previous month in an attempt to work out where I had gone wrong. Germany was much easier to navigate. Some pot-bellied father with a large moustache and a creaky sense of English would ask me why I was orgasming in a PTO meeting. My grammar would be corrected. I would be pointed to the local German language school and advised to learn the language to a level that I would not waste time in future meetings and we would move on. On another occasion I asked for a puppy (Hündchen) in sweet and sour sauce rather than chicken (Hähnchen), and chicken milk cheese (Hühnfrischkäse) rather than chicken fricassee (Hühnerfrikassee) The waitress was a little confused and a conversation followed about how it was not possible to milk a chicken, but eventually, all became clear and it just added to the fun. The Germans did seem to appreciate that I was at least trying to speak the language and, as they got to know us better, would laugh with us rather than at us. This increased the bond and the sense of belonging. There will always be those who will value your correct grammar or spelling more than the sentiment or ideas, revealing their lack of intellect by the narrow measures they choose to use to judge others', but these are the fruits of plastic crates and not those I want to share my wicker basket.

A wonderful free-thinking apricot of a woman was Angelica. She was the German wife of a guy from Worcester rugby club and happily offered to help us in any way she could. Angelica had been born in East Germany and had long mousy hair tied back in a plait that followed her spine down her back to almost her waist. She never wore any makeup, that I remember, and was usually dressed in a heavy metal T-shirt and jeans, all dark in colour. She had a plain appearance, dowdy even, but her smile lit a room. It was the kind of smile that came from deep within her and emanated from her large twinkly brown eyes. It was always there and it welcomed people in making them feel safe and accepted. She may have been raised in the shade of a coconut tree, but her personality was more like the peaches of her newfound country than the hard nuts of the old. She was open and shared her experiences with joy, but you always felt there was a stone hiding a more painful part of her life that she chose to keep to herself. I classify her as an apricot, however, and not a peach because despite the easily penetrated exterior surrounding an impenetrable stone she would never be accepted by the peaches because of the hint of a /v/ in words with a W and the taint of her previous culture which brought judgment.

On a weekend away with the rugby club, she had removed a bath robe before joining the other wives in the sauna and, unconscious of the anxiety nakedness brings to the puritan Americans, was not wearing anything under it. This act brought with it judgment of her moral character and sexual freeness that seemed unsupported by any evidence. After living in Germany, the shock that we too had felt melted into an understanding that for Angelica and Germans nakedness was normal and unconnected to sex.

Each week for the two months before we left, we would drive over to Worcester and sit on the grass on her back garden. As the sun beat down on us and we sipped lemonade and ate picnics she taught us set phrases like, "Can I pay on a credit card?' and "Does your son want to come over and play?", as well as the names of all the foods we had brought over, at her suggestion, to share. She understood what it was like to want to be understood. She knew what it was like when, even if you used the correct words, your place of birth did not afford you the right to share those words. Taxation without representation may have been a reason to fight for independence, but once that independence was secured it was not a right afforded to newly arrived immigrants. Equally, she knew that the country of your birth removed any right to an opinion when you chose to abandon it in search of new adventures. She, like us, was stuck in the culture gap, neither one thing nor the other, accepted by no one, other than other cultural refugees far from home. She listened with understanding and patience as the boys requested essential phrases like, "Help help my belly button is on fire!" and gave me the reassurance that I would be fine. Before my afternoons with Angelica in the garden my only two original phrases of German were, "I love you" and "Will you play with me?"! These were the kinds of phrases that, if used together, may bring judgments on my own moral downfall from the plastic crates of peaches. Angelica gave me the skills to buy a washing machine and buy groceries and most of all she took away the fear. Her glowing smile would be transported with me to a new adventure always telling me, "You can do it. You'll be fine!"

I had longed for a new adventure and new experiences as life evolved into groundhog day, each morning welcoming us to a day almost identical to the previous. The subtle language barrier which had once terrified me in America had now gone as I became excited to take on a new challenge. Growing up my home had been filled with the sound of German, be it in the melodic repetitive tones of a language tape or its contrived sentences being echoed back in my father's deep, broad, Lancashire accent. Occasionally, the tape was replaced by the hard vowels of my uncle's even broader Lancastrian brogue, as he and my father used their newfound language of freedom to discuss whatever they liked, much to the annoyance of my mother and aunt. Here language strengthens the strong bond which united two brothers already bound by the poverty of their humble beginnings and, as my skills grew, I knew my newfound understanding would have been my window into those conversations, peppered with laughter and free from judgment. Sadly they were no longer with us, but it still made me feel a connection, a feeling of a new bond with my roots, cemented my love for this harsh language devoid of tenderness. It also became a language that was to bring frustration, perseverance and most of all laughter.

Do you know that the German words for jockstrap and toad are remarkably similar? Suspensorium and Schildkröte. You don't think they sound anything alike? No neither did the lady in the sports shop, but for some reason, they had been filed away in the same mind drawer in my brain and it was totally hit and miss which one I would pull out at a particular moment in time. When James and I went to buy Henry a jockstrap we were unable to find them so asked the shop assistant in my best German,
"My son will play rugby so I need to buy him a turtle."
"Ein Schildkröte?" she queried.
"Yes, a turtle. He needs a turtle to protect his penis when he plays rugby." "We don't sell turtles that protect penises"
"You do! My friend bought a turtle from here to protect his son's penis this very week. It was white and like a cup that fits over the penis."
She took me to the jockstraps and hopefully, if not desperately, asked if this would be more suitable. She showed me the adult version, but Henry was only five and they were huge so I took a deep breath and said,
"No this will not work. I need a very, very, small turtle to protect his penis".
The woman looked towards James's nether regions with an "Oh dear!" look and pointed at the jockstraps telling me these would be perfect and she had no small turtles.
"No!" I said emphatically. I had learnt by now that to get what you wanted in Germany you needed to be very insistent and refuse to leave until they took you seriously.

If all else failed you threw in the odd, "Das geht nicht!" in a stern voice basically telling them that this will not go and then scowl and give them a Paddington Bear stare. It was a foolproof method.

"Das geht nicht! They are big and my son has a very small penis." She looked at James again and must have thought, however, that he did not need a very, very small one because she again directed me to the very, very big ones and then walked away desperate to escape the mad foreign woman who wanted a Schildkröte. I was about to embark on a chase across the shop floor to go back and tell her again that these were far too big and I definitely needed an extremely small one, but the look on James's face showed me his dignity had been damaged enough so I picked up the smallest one I could find and stitched Henry into it, which made him look like a very big boy! It was only several months later when I discussed with a German friend how I had been walking the dogs and had seen hatchlings in the reeds on the edge of a pond, that I was excited to see them grow into jockstraps that I realised language could be a very big barrier to communication!

If I was to survive I could not be the kind of foreigner who shouted at the locals in English, assuming volume was the main barrier to them understanding my every need. Whilst persistence and a well placed "Das geht nicht" may get me what I wanted it, was not going to help me be accepted and embraced by the community.

Across the road from the children's school was a school where foreigners could learn German. Every morning from 9-12.30 a group of immigrants, most of them refugees escaping atrocities, would pile into the classrooms. The collection of national stereotypes would then be taught German in German by a German. Armando, the Italian, would strut to his desk, always ten minutes after the class had begun, cigarette hanging out of the corner of his mouth. He would nod to reassure us all he had arrived now so we could all begin secure in the knowledge that his presence would enhance our experience. Carla was a Brazilian au pair, with a tiny waist and enormous breasts squashed into a silver top, two or three sizes too small for her, cleavage desperately trying to escape, but framed by long glossy curls of jet black hair. She would glance over at him as she acknowledged her name as the teacher called the register. She would turn her head a little to one side a give him a little pouty smile to show her interest, but he did not notice because his interest was firmly rooted a few inches below her crimson lined lips on the contents of the metallic fabric that was barely constraining her. I sat next to two Moroccan ladies in hijabs, who looked like I may have something in common with as we seemed of a similar age and later discovered this had been a wise choice.

The course was very frustrating to begin with because everyone there had lived there for years and could speak German, but with poor grammar, whereas I was struggling with the basics. Just like Rosetta Stone, we learnt bizarre phrases. Before one test I realised that I could say that my tax accountant farts or was horny, but not that he did my tax return! Again, while doing my German homework translation I could not help, but wonder when I would ever need to know German for torture basement (Folterkeller) again! Still, however, the nuances of the language would escape me at times.

I told a teacher that I would be late the next day because I was going to a party in Edward's German class. Edward was taking lots of gummy bears so, "Morgan, esse ich nur Gummis." As embarrassed giggles emanated from the hijabs on either side of me the teacher, who was accustomed to the faux pas from uneducated immigrants, explained that "gummis" without the accompanying nouns of bears or worms became a noun in itself and I had just told the class that I would only be eating condoms that day!

I learnt in those first few months that being understood is more than sharing a common language. It is about sharing experiences and most of all struggles. On the face of it, I had nothing in common with two muslin women from Morocco. We did not speak the same language, worship the same god, or come from similar backgrounds, but they invited me into their homes, shared the food and shared the struggle of trying to fit in. I had more in common with them than I ever would with the American and British women shouting in English at the Germans trying to make a whole country do it their way. They were peaches and melons trying to turn a whole crate of coconuts into a crate of melons or peaches rather than someone searching for exotic and interesting fruits to join the tropical celebration basket. That was what made them the people who would never understand me whatever language they spoke.

4 FRAU MATILDA THE BEAST OF ACCEPTANCE

Maybe it was the lack of the basics that almost lead to the extermination of poor Matilda. Shortly after we arrived, a letter came which I just kept putting off reading because it looked so difficult and long. I would glance at the "Sehr geehrte Damen und Herren" and even this simple Dear Sir/Madam would fill me with dread, so I would place it back on the ever-increasing pile for yet another day. After putting it off for thirteen days, I finally decided to take on the challenge and it was then that the true horror of a pending doggy holocaust hit me. We had fourteen days to prove that Matilda was of "pure race" or she would be "collected and exterminated!" Visions of cattle trucks heading to doggy concentration camps sprang to mind and we started to make plans to hide her in the attic and buy her a diary. I frantically searched the paperwork we had brought from America, which had also been perpetually put off for another day, and eventually found evidence of her heritage in her pedigree. I rushed down to the town hall with all her papers and she was saved from the gas chamber with only a day to spare!

The holocaust was a dark, dark stain on German history and maybe should not be used so flippantly to talk about a letter about a dog, but the language used was poignant and unchanged from that which had been used to describe the millions of unfortunate jews who suffered at the hands of the Nazis. The word nazi did not seem connected to the lovely natives of our little village who smiled "Guten Morgen" as they passed marching and laughing along the paths through the endless fields, maintaining their well-oiled joints. However, as they left the country paths and headed through the medieval town, through the town gates, on to the cobbles and past the castle, the same feet walked over golden cobbles amongst the grey, each with a name, a date, a place. These were the Stolpersteine that marked where jews affected by the holocaust had lived, when and where they had died. I too had walked over them many times in the first couple of years I was there, never taking the time to look down as I rushed to get an ice cream or meet a friend for lunch or coffee, but now on this day the sun caught the edge of one glistening up at me. I am sure they had glinted in the sun on other days, but this was the day after I had been on a walking tour of Frankfurt for parents at the school and these little stones in the cobbles of the city had been pointed out to us and their significance explained. Now I took notice. I had expected the jews in the city were affected, but naively hadn't thought they would be in our little village. All along the road through the town, stone after stone alerted me to its existence. I read every one and I remembered. All Germans are made to remember in an attempt that they will learn from the past and not repeat it. The holocaust is taught to every child in every school, every year and they are made to feel guilty for their forebears' actions.

In America, things are very different. Every year in November they are not taught of the mass genocide against the Native American's perpetrated by their forebears, but it is taught as a propaganda fairytale where everyone sat together and shared the food they had, so that the brave pilgrims did not starve in their first winter. Rather than learning from the past, it is celebrated with

Thanksgiving turkeys, paper pilgrim hats, and freezing cold games of football.

Britain is no better. We even put a defining adjective before our name making it Great Britain, defining the power that colonising most of the countries of the world, as Great. Children are taught that only 22 countries in existence have never had the benefit of the greatness of the largest empire in history, but a historical amnesia fills those same classrooms like ether when it comes to Boer concentration camps or the Amritsar massacre.

Only when you look in from the outside do you see the propaganda that becomes the cultural norm, allowing judgment of others, free of self-reflection. From the outside looking in this reflection glints of every stone that bears a forgotten soul and reminds us that we are all the same both at a personal and national level and could all benefit from a little more reflection and a little less judgement.

French we were told was the language for your wife, Italian for your lover, English for business and German for your dog. Maybe this is why, after the shaky start, Frau Matilda embraced German culture with all four paws and after dinner would sit and bark until we took her to the pub for a pint.

They loved Matilda as she loved their beer gardens lined with bits of discarded schnitzel and sausage. She was immediately accepted when we arrived, but the locals took a little longer to warm to the rest of us. As I have already said our cultural trainer told us that Germans were like coconuts and it was tough to get through the outer shell, but once you made it through they totally opened up to you. This did seem to be the case.

A few days after we arrived, we went to the local ice-cream

shop. It was on the main street in the town in one of the lovely black and white timbered buildings that looked like they had been there for all eternity. Outside metal tables and chairs tumbled out on to the streets some sporting large umbrellas to add a little shade. We found the only free table and sat down and I asked in my very best German, courtesy of Angelica, for a strawberry, a vanilla and two chocolate ice-creams. It wasn't that difficult and I was quite proud of myself until the arrogant waiter shouted at the top of his voice in German, "What do you want?" He then turned to the rest of the patrons sitting under the umbrellas and asked, "Was sagt deise Frau? Ich kann sie nicht verstehen!" He smiled and nodded at his audience as if to assert that he was part of them and I was not, as he ran a hand through his thick black hair. A lady on the next table glanced over at me and smiled reassuringly as she repeated what I had just said and then turned to me and told me that I was perfectly easy to understand and complimented me on my German. Her reassurance allowed all the muscles in my body that had tensed up a few minutes earlier to relax back against my aluminium chair. Her smile meant that, rather than dreading going into a hostile town, I could pluck up the courage to try again and again to fit in. She probably forgot about what had happened as she left the table and headed down the cobbles and through the arch of the clocktower to her car, but I didn't forget.

By the time we left three years later the ice-cream seller, who himself was not German, seemed to have accepted us entirely and welcomed us with open arms. I, however, never totally forgot the day he chose to embarrass me in front of half of the town and use me as a shield against his own insecurities, throwing me to the lions to gain his own acceptance. Some people, normally those who have experienced unfamiliar surroundings, have empathy for the struggles of those battling for a place of acceptance whilst others cling to like souls deflecting the newly arrived. He may have decided I was now to be allowed into the inner circle of his Eis cafe, but I had not welcomed him into my basket of like souls and his tips would never be what I would call substantial!

If there was ever to be any form of discrimination it always excluded Matilda and was aimed firmly at the two-legged members of the family. When we went to one restaurant with Matilda we asked for a table and they welcomed us in until they saw we had three young children and then bluntly told us that the dog was welcome, but with three kids, the rest of us needed to find somewhere else to eat! Some restaurants even had a reserved sign on the tables, even though nobody had reserved them. This allowed the owner to vet you before giving you a table and on many occasions, the lack of revenue was preferable to us. Some tables even had a sign that blatantly let you know that you were being discriminated against. The Stammtisch table was reserved for locals only and often stood empty as we were sent away hungry. In the last six months of our three years we were granted a seat on the Stammtisch and, at that point, knew we had been accepted. I felt no warmth in this acceptance though. It had come with a trail by exclusion for the previous two years and so was not a place I wanted to be. It was like being asked to leave a tropical fruit basket sitting on a party table to finally be allowed in the old plastic crate of identical fruits rotting away on the dock. In America, there was no trial by exclusion. We were considered acceptable immigrants and always invited to join the locals sometimes feeling like the entertainment or prized new possession, but this just shows the ridiculous nature of prejudice.

Our favourite restaurant was La Table. They welcomed all of us, Matilda and the kids, with open arms. I would try to tie her up outside, but they would insist that she came into the tiny cafe where she filled the white tiled floor and made the waitresses jump over her like show jumping ponies to deliver the food to the half a dozen or so tables with tablecloths covered in pink and blue hydrangeas. One day, shortly after arriving in Germany, I went there with my new friend Laurie and her two children. She had just been to the shops and had bought an enormous courgette which she placed on the table next to the delicate china teacups. As the food arrived we realised that the table was far too small for seven of us and a humongous zucchini so, as another table was vacated, the waitress suggested we moved, allowing us to spread out a little. We jumped at the chance and Laurie leapt up, courgette in hand, to claim the table before anyone else came into the tiny cafe. The sleeping Matilda awoke with a start as Laurie's right leg stretched over her back towards the larger table. Before Laurie's left leg could follow, Matilda stood up making Laurie have to fight to maintain her balance as she straddled the 120 pounds of terrified Newfoundland. As Laurie's left hand clung on to the table, her right arm waved in a circular movement, still clutching the colossal green vegetable. Matilda looked around for a place to escape the zucchini welding rodeo star, but she was hemmed in by tables and screaming children. Her big brown eyes looked at me begging for help and eventually I managed to free myself from behind the table and steady her long enough for Laurie's left leg to rejoin her right, allowing her to securely place the courgette on the table and take a seat. The waitress placed our food on the table with a gentle "Alles gut" and nothing else was said. You would think this level of disruption to a "ladies who lunch" kind of cafe would mean we were all banned and that Matilda and her courgette welding jockey would definitely not manage to find an unreserved table ever again. However, the little cafe, filled with German ladies wrapped in pashminas, huge diamonds glinting on their fingers, positively encouraged us to return. From that day both La Table and Laurie were to become two of my most favourite things in Germany.

Laurie was the zucchini in my celebration fruit basket, placing herself firmly in the centre with a rye smile and a wink, alerting you to the phallic nature of her position next to a couple of ripe plums. Laurie would not be seen dead in a plastic crate of identical fruits and, to be honest, it would be difficult to know in which crate to place her. Born and raised in Michigan she was living with an Irishman in Germany with her Finnish children and told stories of her time with the Peace Corp in Kyrgyzstan and teaching in Finland, Malawi, Bahrain, Taiwan, Northern Ireland, and Germany. She seemed to speak every language known to man and play an array of musical instruments. Every meeting with Laurie revealed a new hidden talent, or even more outrageous story and her "try anything" attitude led me to places I would never have dreamt of exploring and experiences I would never have dared to try.

Dominic, like Matilda, also took to the German way of life very easily and, once he realised that you could drink a beer in the cinema at 11 am whilst watching Ice Age and sitting in the biggest seat I've ever seen, I wondered if he would ever move back to the States. Worryingly even little Henry began to feel alcohol was an important part of his life. On one occasion I bought him a doughnut at the supermarket as a treat and when he had eaten half of it the lady behind the counter laughed as she told me the high alcohol content would help him sleep tonight. On another occasion friends, who were also teachers at his school, took him to a neighbour's party and it was only after he and their son had each drunk three large glasses of fruit punch that they realised that it was actually rum punch.

Germany had a relaxed attitude to alcohol which was in stark contrast to the Land of the Free, where the drinking age was 21, which was still quite shocking from my British perspective. Children, in Germany, would work at the festivals where Henry earned a few cents by collecting up beer bottles while older children were put to work pulling pints in the beer tent. When we eventually returned to the US I found out teachers had raised concerns about our parenting skills when Henry was given the Massachusetts Health Survey to complete. He had raised his hand and asked for help answering the question which asked if he had ever drunk more than just a sip of alcohol. He was not sure what he should put since he had been "knocking back rum punch since the age of four", but it was "legal in Germany". He failed to inform the teacher that it was only on one occasion, his parents were not present because he was with two teachers from his school and the whole thing was an accident. His recollections of his misspent youth were only made worse since the teacher, he recounted them to, was the same teacher to whom I had said, "I could kill him" the week before when I found his lost math homework, that everyone had been searching high and low for three days, was actually in the bottom of the lego bucket. As many Americans take everything literally this meant that I was actually concerned social services would be knocking at the door as she had asked for advice on how to respond to my threats of infanticide.

Alcohol was part of life in Germany. Festivals were family affairs and the community came together over a beer, with a drinking song or two and a stroll back home through the fields. In America alcohol was taboo. Kids drank secretly in basements and dorm rooms and then drove back home too scared to tell their parents they should not really be driving. Many parents too had a laissez fair attitude to drink driving which would make you a social outcast in Europe.

Never, however, was the true horror of excessive drinking more evident than at the annual Kerb in Germany, a festival that still seems outrageous to me even after surviving three of them.

5 NEVER DISCUSS ENGELBERT HUMPERDINCK OVER A SCHLAMBOWLE!

Every year in May, the whole town stopped for a huge festival which lasted five days. In the weeks, before it began, sixteen-year-old boys would be taken by the older men from the church in the middle of town into the woods. Here they would be taught drinking songs and collected small saplings which they cut down, added a red ribbon and sold to people in the town to strap to their gate posts. As the event grew closer a huge beer tent would appear, filling most of the car park in the centre of town. A couple of days before, the tent would be joined by fairground rides and food trucks selling everything from sweet treats to the obligatory sausage. The start of the Kerb was marked by a procession of boys all wearing white shirts, sashes over their shoulders, straw hats covered in flowers and a beer glass tied around their neck, hanging from red ribbons.

As they arrived at the lake by the castle a whole host of horrors awaited them. Firstly, they would be expected to climb a telegraph pole to sit on a chair strapped to the top. If they survived this, which inevitably they all seemed to do, they would be dunked in the lake in a kind of ritual baptism. Looking on were large groups of men of various ages, each group wearing matching T-shirts sporting the year they had been one of the boys to have survived the initiation ceremonies. Benches were adorned by three or four grey-haired men in T-shirts sporting, "Kerb 1949", looking on silently taking it all in as they had done for the last sixty years. A group of thirty or so middle aged men ,with stomachs that had seen the benefit of a pint or two over the years since their Kerb in 1984, stood reliving their youth, pretending for a night or two that they did not have the responsibilities of a kid climbing the obligatory pole. Their offspring were either dressed in the white shirts and flowery hats or wearing a T-shirt with Kerb two thousand and something or were acting as slave labour in the beer tent, where only the young were sober and responsible enough to take charge. Their wives stood by matching them pint for pint, but looking a little more glamorous in their brightly coloured dirndls. It seemed like wherever you ended up in life if you had grown up in Dreieichenhein, you returned each May, like swallows in the spring, or a repetitive, drunken Preston Guild.

That afternoon the town erupted into a riotous drinking festival filled with lederhosen, dirndls, Oompah bands and beer. It was so much fun the first year we were there. It was the night that Engelbert Humperdinck represented the UK in the Eurovision song contest. We stayed in the town all day and as the night drew in and the local cafes closed, the choice of drinks grew less. Beer was the main offering, but if you did not want beer the only other offering was a Schlammbowle. This was a rich, creamy, smoothie, laced with vodka and whatever other spirits they seemed to have lying around which seemed to totally remove any ability I had to speak in coherent sentences. Not to be defeated, I spent the whole night overcoming its debilitating powers which prevented me from saying, Engelbert Humperdinck. The more I tried the more Schlammbowles I had and the worse it became, which became more and more amusing to me. That night Dominic decided to walk his friend Barry and Barry's bike home because he was worried that they were so intoxicated that they could not make it home alone.

Barry lived on the first floor of a block of flats which had no lift, but Dominic managed to get both Barry and the bike home safely and tuck them both up in bed together, Barry and the bike! Luckily Barry had some terrible bedroom habit, which we never totally were privy too, that meant he and his wife Marion had separate rooms so it was not until the following morning that Marion was to be made aware of the horror which slept in the adjacent room. The following morning was less fun for everyone than the night before, with many sore heads and broken glass and vomit adorning the town streets, yet none of this seemed to prevent it all being repeated the following afternoon and evening. As the week progressed the sounds of oompah bands pulsed through your body into the small hours of the morning, even when led in bed far from the festivities. Night after night after night, the lack of sleep and total exhaustion this resulted in meant that the whole Kerb thing began to wear a bit thin. We longed to just be able to drift off to sleep with the faint hum of distant traffic rather than to the sound of a town full of drunk Germans singing Zehn Kleine Jägermeister accompanied by a french horn, trombone and accordion!

America's attitudes to alcohol was much more puritan. Drinking was something to be hidden, almost something to be ashamed of. You could not drink outside in public spaces so cans and bottles were hidden in coolers and poured into plastic cups. The drinking age was 21, which meant that kids drank in secret in basements and dorm rooms far from the protection of a pub landlord or the community in general and then, keen to keep the secret, they would drive home. We told our kids that they must follow the law of the country they were in and if they didn't agree with it they needed to campaign to change the law. They knew that drink driving would not be accepted and that no questions would be asked if we ever had a late night phone call to go and collect them or a friend who should have been the designated driver. Drinking and driving did not have the stigma that it did in Europe and it was common for adults and teenagers alike to get in the car intoxicated. This was the land of contradictions where drinking a glass of wine with dinner was apparently a bigger threat to a twenty year old's health than the risk of being hit by an adult arrogant enough to think that they could drive drunk. These contradictions made understanding this attitude difficult for international children like mine.

When Edward returned to the States and had a lesson on the dangers of drugs and alcohol on the teenage brain, he used the Kerb to illustrate how the teachers' insistence, that alcohol damaged young brains irreversibly, made no sense since all Germans are not brain damaged. He told her it was a church-run event in May where the whole town came together to teach sixteen year olds "how to drink". The arrogance of adults told him he was wrong as she confused the Kerb with Octoberfest. Frustrated he returned home and asked me to email her. I explained that although it did sound strange to an American's ears, he was telling the truth. Her email back aggressively told me that her wisdom was not to be questioned so I just told Edward to keep his mouth shut in her class and wait for the end of the year. A couple of months later in the parent teacher conference, she told us how Edward had stopped participating in class. When I explained to her that I had just told him to keep his head down, she went a very bright shade of purple and yelled, "I was very offended by your email. My husband is black you know and my children are biracial!" I wasn't entirely sure of the significance of a black husband unless he was German, but her rant continued for a little while and then Dominic and I suggested we should leave and the conference ended. We showed the principal her emails and he agreed she was in the wrong and we moved on.

Her mind was closed to the idea that others may have a different set of rules. She believed that having an interracial marriage meant that she was 'other' and I am sure that her life was full of experiencing being the outsider, but her attitude was still that of a peach in a crate of peaches. She did not appreciate that others may be outsiders in a different way than she was, and did not appreciate that people may just do things differently. They were not necessarily wrong or right, just different. My children had a wider view of life that meant they may not see things in the same way or interpret her questions in the way that everyone else had always done.
This made me realise that it was not a shared experience of being the outsider that earned you a place in my celebration fruit basket, but how you accepted other outsiders. It was not enough to try and hide your own difference and blend in, you needed to embrace variety.

In Germany, the couple of families from the American Midwest, believed themselves to be mavericks, travelling for a two year stint in Germany far from the comforts of Walmart, but when they arrived they clumped together and searched for familiar peanut butter and waxy Hershey's kisses. It was the same in America, when the Brits invaded hunting for sausage and refusing to use the word restroom. They moved to experience another country and absorb all the riches that affords you, but then made a little enclave of their own country devoid of the character of their new land, expecting the locals to change too. We all want the comfort of the familiar, to hang on to our own culture and traditions. When we arrived in America my children had closets full of nationalistic T-shirts and trousers emblazoned with union jacks and the three lions of the England football team. I was driven by a fear of losing my identity, but did not realise that that identity was so much more than a flag or a football team. My identity would evolve as I became international, not British, a nationality that had no government to protect me and no passport to identify me.

This blatant disregard for local culture was never more evident than Halloween in Germany. Halloween was not a German tradition, but still, all the American children in the school would gather together and wander the streets knocking on doors shouting "trick or treat" to the bemused Germans who would try to figure out what they were supposed to do. On one occasion one threw a tub of humous into the waiting bucket. At this time of year, German children would go door to door with paper lanterns lit by a little battery operated bulb and sing songs that glorify St. Martin's act of sharing. Even in England where Halloween was a little more common, children dressed as ghosts and witches, but not as Captain America or a Disney princess. This kind of Halloween was a purely American phenomenon. When nobody answered the door or came devoid of treats for the waiting hoard the American parents started to complain.
"Why did they leave a light on if they had nothing?" "Why do they have decorations if they weren't going to be in?" The answer was simple, because they don't celebrate Halloween and they don't want to sit in the dark all night because some foreigners can't understand that the whole world has chosen to do something differently. They had their own festivals and many of those seemed strange to outsiders, but that was what makes living somewhere else interesting, looking into others' crates and taking away what you love for your own. We still fill our children's shoes with chocolate for Nikolaus, burn candles on the Weihnacht pyramid, burn a guy on the bonfire for Guy

Fawkes, egg roll at Easter, celebrate the war we lost on July 4th and a dinner that probably never happened on Thanksgiving. As we melt the Bleigiessen on New Years' Eve to predict our future and we feel blessed that we have enveloped the festivals of all three countries into our family's traditions.

There were so many festivals to enjoy, where you could fit into the local culture rather than jutting up against it, be it the Fasching Karneval where James wore a toilet seat around his neck, waved a loo brush and fitted in perfectly or the renaissance festival where naked people ran to grab a sausage, again looking totally normal, unlike Captain America and Ariel on a cold Halloween night.

I loved the Renaissance festival and it was by far my favourite event of the year. Folk music would echo around the walls of the castle as men in Kilts beat drums and played bagpipes, or heavy rock folk groups made noises that felt like the vibrations would turn the thousand year old mortar between the old stones to dust. The noises pulsated through you as you stood and listened, rooting you to the ground and making you feel part of the environment. People came from far and wide to sell their handcrafted jewellery, medieval weapons, dresses, hats and pots. You saw things on stalls that you did not normally see and it was reminiscent of the traders meeting at the crossroads of trading routes for centuries before. The food was fantastic. Whole fish nailed to boards smoked over open fires, the pink flesh of the salmon turning darker in the smoky fumes which laced your clothes with the scent of yesteryear. Pigs turned on spits, their outer skin turning a rich brown which glistened as it became crispier and crispier and sausages sizzled with onions and peppers waiting to be stuffed into soft white rolls with tangy sauces. Beer of cause was everywhere and any other drinks needed to be searched out on stalls with crepes or candy floss where they were an almost forgotten incidental. As the stalls went up, a giant barrel about ten or twelve feet in diameter would also arrive under a large oak tree in the corner of the car park in the middle of town. As the stalls around it filled with assorted wares and food trucks filled in the gaps, the bath was filled with water using a huge pipe. At first, we wondered if there would be animals and this was their source of drinking water, but as we wandered down the cobbled street on the first day of the festival all became clear.   Around the edge of the barrel were hairy beasts of a whole different kind. Naked Germans lined the oak slats, their arms intertwined along its rim, their modesty remaining intact with the mirky waters that skimmed just above the pendulous breasts of the ladies of the group. We wandered over to a calligraphy stall where a lady in a blue woollen dress that reached down to her ankles and was tied at the waist with a golden yellow chord, sat quill in hand. As she started to show us how to write our names in black ink on crisp yellowing parchment paper with the quill pen, she glanced up to see a man with a long brown beard and hairy chest jump out of the barrel and hop over to the smoked salmon stall, the towel, that could have hidden his meat and two veg, hiding nothing but the shoulder it was draped over. She looked down at the letters now appearing beautifully on the page and muttered in her soft Scottish accent "He'd be put on a register where I'm from"

6 THE NAKED TRUTH

What is your taboo? Is it the same as my taboo? Were you born with that taboo and will it stay with you throughout your life? I would propose that our taboos are different and evolve. We are not born with them, but they are bestowed on us by our culture and those significant in our lives. They change when the significant people in our life change and are shaped by the actions of those in our community. For those who stay in the same community with the same people shaping their thoughts these taboos will probably remain constant. They won't even think of them as unique to their culture, assuming the same views are shared by all those in the civilised world, but this is not true. Taboos are a cultural phenomenon and as you move from one culture to another you begin to question them and see the absurdity they create, yet still, they are so important to acceptance you cannot ignore them. Nakedness was part of life in Germany. It was not a taboo. It was not something they even thought about until they were greeted by the shocked face of their transatlantic visitors and then they would just laugh at the absurdity of the puritan Americans for whom the naked human body was most definitely taboo. This created conflict since taboos are not to be questioned.

I first realised this when we were instructed to buy swimming attire by the school, very small, tight, navy blue speedos, budgie smugglers as Dominic referred to them! The newly arrived American parents were horrified! They discussed how the school was culturally unaware and that this was totally unacceptable. As time went on they would realise that they had bigger things to worry about as they inadvertently signed permission slips for a school trip to the local brothel and were confronted with sex education in almost every year from preschool to 9th grade, at which point it was assumed all pupils had lost their virginity so additional instruction was now redundant. The anxiety of the budgie smugglers seemed to be passed on to their offspring since parents informed the school that their children were having difficulty sleeping, consumed by the worries of displaying the silhouette their meat and two veg in the new attire. My boys were less anxious and I realised that I had raised kids with high self-esteem when one emerged from the Decathlon changing room informing the whole shop floor that he could "pull this off" because he had "a small bum and big crown jewels." All of this was set to the soundtrack of his younger brother gyrating his hips as he pranced around the shoe section devoid of shoes, but happily wearing nothing, but his new budgie smugglers singing "I'm sexy and I know it!" All the kids soon learned to adapt and the parents soon moved on to the next cultural juxtaposition to become anxious about.

Even on our trip to check things out we had been shocked to be swimming in the hotel pool, splashing around and perfecting our synchronised swimming routines, when suddenly out of nowhere appeared a totally naked German pensioner, towel thrown over his shoulder as he bent over at the drinking fountain to reveal his butt hole its full glory. Did he have dementia? Was he a pervert? So many questions flashed through my puritan mind as I worried about the safety of my children, with only me to protect them in the otherwise empty pool. Soon, however, we were not alone as a whole group formed around the fountain, pendulous bosoms joining sagging bum cheeks each with a towel concealing only a wrinkled shoulder. The sheer number suggested no individual perversion and brought with it a reassurance that we were safe. This was confirmed the following day by Gabi our relocation specialist who informed us it would just have been "special evening". What we had seen was definitely not special and, once we began regularly visiting the outdoor pool in the summer, we realised that this was something which was in no way confined to the evenings. As we sat on the grass around the pool checking over, now and again, to see whether the kids had drowned or not, our view would often be obscured by grown men in business suits stripping off to reveal a large hairy bottom, which seemed always to be pointing in my direction. The huge, hairy posterior was then wriggled into some tiny, silky, blue speedos which resembled more of a thong than any swimming regalia I had ever seen. The wearer would then inevitably turn to face me before adjusting his crown jewels and then bringing relief to the eyes as he jumped into the cool, concealing waters for a swim. He would have no embarrassment and be totally unaware of mine, since this was how it was in Germany. Bodies were bodies. Not sexual in any way unless you had other predetermined plans. Nakedness and sex were, to the Germans, two separate entities, unlike the Americans who seemed to see the two concepts as always one.

Even school trips for kindergarteners were fraught with danger. Henry was at that age where he had not developed any inhibitions and where body parts were the funniest thing in the world and penises seemed to come up in every conversation from questions as to whether or not sausages were 'pigs willies" to discussions about how putting silly bands on your man sausage may cause it to drop off. I definitely regretted telling him that one on the day I told him to push into my lap to help put his boot on and he said, "You mean where your willy used to be?"

"No" I said "I'm a girl I've never had a willy."

"Trust me" was his reply "You did you just played with it too much and it dropped off!"

Any confusion on the female form would definitely be explored and fully resolved on his trip to Explora Museum. As the bus pulled up at the museum of visual illusions, as it had been described on the consent form, there would be plenty of opportunities to examine the differences between the male and female forms in glorious technicolour and 3D. There would be plenty of opportunities for the American Kindergarten teacher to regret not checking the museum out before she brought the whole class and their puritan parent chaperones for a visit!

The excited children alighted the bus and skipped over to play in the playground and enjoy their last few moments of innocence before the museum opened. As the clock struck ten they were rounded up and herded in to see what the educational facility had to offer. We stood in the foyer and one teacher purchased the tickets and met our guide the other teacher looked at the huge picture of Sigmund Freud on the wall next to her. His high forehead sloped down to two thick black eyebrows above his deep set eyes and the profile perspective of the picture highlighted his hooked nose on which wire rimmed spectacles were perched and his thick very bushy beard. She was just about to explain to the children who Freud was and ask them to look at the picture when she looked a little more intensely and noticed that Freud was in fact made up of naked women and his eyebrow was, actually, a thick bushy clump of pubic hair resting above the bent provocative leg which made up his nose. She quickly stood with her back to it obscuring the delights of his bushy beard from view as a host of six year olds battled to see the now intensely interesting poster. This was not the only piece of art she would obscure that morning as she would spend a lot of her day with her back to pieces of art wishing she had checked out the museum first! The whole museum was filled with what first appeared to be innocent artwork, but turned out to be pictures of numerous sexual acts some which were even an education to me. Naked bodies twisted into unimaginable positions to reveal their full glory and I will never forget the sight of three six year old boys stood in a row, backpacks clinging to their backs, staring at a picture in their 3D glasses, mouths wide open, eyes unblinking, amazed by what they saw, whilst a horrified first grade teacher tried in vain to encourage them to move on.

To the Germans, this was not an inappropriate school trip. The museum was full of young minds open to new sights and concepts. Germans did not think of an unclothed body any differently than a clothed one. It was an educational experience both in visual illusions and in sex. To Germans, this education started in preschool and was no different from Maths or English. Nakedness was normal.

When the bicycle part of the heart ultrasound machine broke during an appointment, it would not have entered anyone's head to cover up my naked boobs, glistening in the bright halogen lights, smeared in KY jelly. Why would you need to cover me up before bringing in the entire hospital maintenance team with toolboxes full of screwdrivers and spanners? As they tightened up nuts and undid screws and discussed between themselves how to resolve the problem, nobody even considered that I would feel uncomfortable and the longer I lived there the less uncomfortable I felt in such situations until, for me too, it was normal. You become desensitised and it becomes liberating.

Britain sits somewhere between the two extremes of America and Germany. When I first moved to the States I remember thinking it strange that kids didn't run on the sand on the beach naked, jumping in and out of the waves, unhindered by soggy wet swim shorts and sequinned swimsuits. I never understood why American TV shows about giving birth would be a series of screens of pixillated images, with only the mother's screams and a scarce narration to allow you to figure out what was going on. I had now lived in America long enough to have become resensitised to nudity, making this an even more difficult transition than if I had come directly from England. Nudity had become abnormal to me and shocking, maybe not to the extent it shocked an American, but it seemed out of the norm. After three years in Germany, I became desensitised and it again became something unremarkable.

When I returned to America and suggested during a mammogram that I just took the gown off completely and placed it on the chair instead of putting one arm back in and then the other, manoeuvring fabric to cover my modesty, the woman who spent her whole day squashing boobs between glass plates, was horrified. She told me it would make her feel uncomfortable. I wanted to tell her that if the sight of naked breasts made her feel uncomfortable she had picked the wrong job, but instead, I awkwardly continued with the ridiculous time consuming performance of covering up the newly released boob so she could squash the other one like a German buttock in a speedo. It seemed strange how being absorbed in another culture could twist your perceptions one way and then twist them back to their original position and then back through to the other extreme again. None of this was conscious and it did not happen with all aspects of life just some. It made me question which cultural norms are so deeply entrenched that you never adjust and which are still malleable. I never adjusted to the American view of education, in which regurgitating predetermined facts, devoid of critical thinking, was acceptable, but nudity was something where I adapted to the crowd. What was it about one that made it fixed and the other that made it amorphous? Did the peaches, trying to change the crate of coconuts, see everything as fixed and what made you a changeable or a fixed person? I still don't know the answer, but I learnt what I was prepared to adapt to and what for me was sacred.

I never totally became as comfortable as the Germans though and this was never any clearer than when my appendages again experienced a taste of the difference in cultures when we went to the Black Forest. We chose a relaxing hotel with a spa and I booked massages for both me and Edward. I was first greeted by a skinny lady with a soft voice who booked me in and asked me to take a seat. The time came for my massage and the same lady asked me to follow her to the room. How I loved those rooms! Small and dark with a heated bed in the middle and the lovely smell of the oils. Maybe the sound of a water feature in the background or the gentle ping ping music or sounds of whales calling to one another. On the bed would be soft blankets or crisp sheets they asked you to lie under as they left to allow you to undressed. Imagine then the shock as she opened the door to a very large room with huge uncurtained picture windows overlooking the hotel garden and an Indian man, who I was sure I had seen fixing a door earlier in the day, waiting there for me. The lady with the soft voice left and the Indian man asked me to undress whilst he stood mixing up some oils. He seemed to have forgotten to leave the room or ask me to get under the crisp sheet, let alone pull the curtains to make it darker or even to turn on the ping ping music. In fact, closer inspection revealed he had totally forgotten to put any sheet for me to hide under anywhere in the room! I manage to remove all the clothes except my knickers very quickly and lie face down on the bed in the centre of the room. What followed was like no massage I've ever had before! The lack of a sheet to hide my dignity was the least of my worries. When he said full body he really meant it! He only missed a central two inch strip of one's lady garden and did things to my appendages that even a husband should ask before attempting!. I kept having the urge to say, "I'm British you know we don't do nudity", but in that very British way, I decided not to make a fuss. As I left the room, however, I whispered to Edward, "keep your pants on" as he entered for his massage! This seemed to be the norm because in the next hotel we stayed in, following my experience with the Indian odd job man, a stern Eastern European lady gave my boobs a good seeing to with a couple of scrubbing brushes! Needless to say, I decided not to have anymore massages in Germany.

I had always worried that we looked strange to Americans because we were coming from such different places. We may not have had a skin colour that alerted them to our alien status, but as Henry's bare bum reversed out of the bathroom in Starbucks for "checking" whilst his brother loudly sang, "sticks and stones may break my bones but chains and whips excite me" we definitely did not look like locals. I had grown up in a house where nobody covered up and my kids had been raised that there was nothing unusual about a parent wandering from the bedroom to the bathroom naked, but I soon realised that this was not normal to most Americans. They covered up even within the family and after the age of five public nudity became illegal. Your six year old desperate for a wee could not wee on a grass verge and breastfeeding in public was frowned upon. When we first moved to America, it was technically illegal. These were all traps I could easily have fallen into. Germany on the other hand was easy. Everything seemed ok and it was difficult to break the rules when it came to nudity.

Sausage Island was the perfect example of the relaxed attitude this rules orientated country, of Germany, had to the human form. Looking for an alternative to the local pool with its budgie smuggling businessmen we were introduced to Sausage Island by a teacher from the boys' school and their family. We shook out our picnic blanket and settled down on the grass which overlooked a large oval-shaped lake with an island in the middle. A beach lined the whole circumference of the lake and a thick privet hedge with a gate seemed to separate it into two distinct zones, although everyone was free to pass from one zone to the other and it was easy to swim between them. As we paddled in the water you could feel large, brown, dappled fish brush against your legs which was unnerving, but the water was clear enough to see them swimming around your feet which brought the reassurance of unpolluted waters. A little snack shack sold the obligatory sausage and schnitzels and drinks and ice creams and, as the parents drank beer and tucked into the sausage, we assumed the venue had got its colloquial name from the snacks and this island. The boys finished their ice creams and decided to go for a swim. They asked if they could try to swim to the island in the middle of the lake and, since they were strong swimmers and we could see the rough outline of sunbathers on the island laying under the shade of the trees, we told them to enjoy themselves. When they later returned we discovered that the island was in easy reach of both beaches in the two distinct zones around the lake. We discovered that they had spoken to Mr. Simmons an English teacher at their school and that he had decided to swim there from the other beach, the nudist beach! We also discovered why the island had got its name and that Mr. Simmons had been browning his sausage very nicely on the island!

7 A VERY BROAD EDUCATION

Mr. Simmons was typical of international school teachers. To pack up and move to another country to teach and, in most cases go from place to place, was a sign of a wild and wandering spirit and many international teachers were unusual characters, to say the least. Added to that was the fact that most international schools are private schools and not constrained by local authorities and government rules. They were businesses and like all businesses needed to protect their reputation. The heady mix of wild, eccentric mavericks as teachers and a need to cover up any scandal which these characters would inevitably create was a dangerous mix.

When Professor Boule arrived to take up his post as the new principle he spent all his time in his office, obviously making plans for moving the school forward. Alarm bells should have started to ring when he emerged from his office to watch a group of thirteen year olds practising for the upcoming musical. He congratulated the girls, all dressed as cheerleaders, who had just performed a dance, saying that they would all be able to get jobs in the Moulin Rouge when they left school. I am sure the parents of these girls each paying 20,000 plus euros were hoping for a greater return on their daughter's education than becoming a topless dancer in a Paris nightclub.

After his little faux pas, he disappeared back into his office, but his real activities were soon to be revealed by a group of seven to nine year olds who were receiving a more advanced education than was probably appropriate from Professor Boule, soon to be renamed Professor Boobs. Professor Boobs corner office backed on to the playground and had large picture windows which filled the upper two thirds of the two outer walls, flooding his office with natural light. As he sat at his desk, with his back to the very large windows they offered him very little privacy. The whole school was very open and offered maximum visibility. It was owned by a kitchen manufacturer called Mr. Hoff who had set the school up to increase his profile in the community and, it was claimed, to act as a tax loophole. Each classroom had a wall of glass separating it from the corridor which was floored with grey granite. None of this was set up for the benefit of its pupils, who were from Frankfurt's wealthiest and most prestigious families. Ambassadors' children, bankers' children, all high profile targets, if you were that way inclined. All being educated in glass classrooms with nowhere to hide with an open door policy of people wandering in and out often meeting Mr. Hoff for conferences and business meetings, he would organise to take part at school. Little feet would slip on the wet granite and bang their heads against the stone steps. The purpose of the school seemed not to educate, but to feed Mr. Hoff's ego and provide a place for the not very bright children of his cronies to go to, to avoid the shame of the Grund Schule when they failed the exam for the gymnasium.

Professor Boobs was not spending hours on his computer in his corner office planning for a better education. He was not aware that the children were peering over his shoulder. He was not aware that they would report in detail what they had seen on his computer to their parents. James had viewed similar content on the computer of the boy sat in front of him in class and was very distressed as he came home with reports of "gentleman's literature" on the boy's computer. The parents of the children who had seen such content on Professor Boobs's computer probably did not need Edward's clarification that, gentleman's literature meant pictures of a gentleman watering a lady garden, as their little darlings had used less colloquial terms to describe what they had seen. When confronted by the parents, Professor Boobs, said he was only doing research on carnivals in Rio for an activity he was planning for the school, but when it was suggested that a parent, who worked in IT, said he could confirm this with a forensic examination of Professor Boobs computer, he decided to promptly leave the school and find another position.

Edward, therefore, knew it all long before his American school broached the subject, because he had covered it all five years earlier in Germany. In preparation for his German sex ed, Edward and his friend Conor decided to discuss what was on the horizon in their next Biology lesson with an English busty blonde teacher called Ms. Grafton. I listened in to their conversation as Edward enquired, "Well I know what to stick where, but that only takes two seconds so what else is she going to talk about for the whole semester? We did all the plant stuff. Remember when Ramiro googled "plant sex" and there was all that funny stuff with a pineapple or cucumber or something". My heart bled for the poor girl who ended up with either of these clueless boys and I wondered if Miss Grafton would be pointing out it may be best to leave the pineapple in the fruit bowl and discuss some technique to make it last a little longer than two minutes! ·

We realised that sex education was a yearly event in Germany because, despite being two years above Edward,

James seemed to be covering it too. His year however, having already covered pineapples, cucumbers and the basics, had moved on to the dangers that you may encounter on the journey to sexual liberation. As he bent himself into the front seat of the tiny red mini, we had bought before they all exploded in height, he informed me that he "had mono, but all the boys at the back of the class had sexually transmitted diseases," but that "Navid's dad was a penis doctor so he would help." It turned out they were discussing infections and he obviously learnt something because the next day he came home showed us a page full of very interesting pictures and told us that the one he was pointing at was the worst one because you grow mushrooms in your vagina. With some closer inspection, I was able to point out that AIDS, chlamydia, and gonorrhoea are all a bit worse than thrush!

Expectations of the education system are, again, a cultural phenomenon. We assume that everyone wants the best education for their child which is probably correct, but we also make assumptions about what that education would be. America lurks down at the bottom of most international league tables for education, yet any discussion of how it could be improved was again a taboo. People in Massachusetts would reassure themselves with the unsubstantiated belief that they were, "not like the rest of America" and nothing should change. Homework was not marked instead teachers used the excuse that they marked on effort not correctness to defend their neglect of this important part of their job. "We don't have time to mark homework" they declared in the same breath as "we are one of the best school districts you know?" The lack of critical thinking and inability to substantiate or question facts seemed to be handed from one generation to the other. Many Americans don't question. America is the best and if you never leave your own backyard you have no reason to believe otherwise. The large swathes of Indian computer programmers and European managers who were moving into their communities were coming to find better lives. They were being headhunted because American schools were failing to teach math and science effectively and not teaching and encouraging the out of the box problem solving needed to effectively manage large organisations. The Education system was blind to its failings. Worse still when Americans moved to Germany they tried to change that system to match the one they had left with marks being given for right or wrong not creativity. They demanded a rubric for everything as though life would always come with a rubric. James saw the difference immediately declaring that European Math was fun, unlike American Math. Suddenly, instead of a page of sixty repetitive problems that required you to plug numbers in like a robot, he had math problems of increasing difficulty which required him to think critically. They may have taken him twice as long, but they were fun and required him to have understanding.

Being part of an international community brought even more wonderful opportunities for learning, allowing you to delve into new ways of thinking, new ways to do familiar tasks. A Japanese friend taught us to use an abacus and a Dutch friend introduced me to the concept of mindset and motivation. This enriched our lives because we allowed it to. Those trying to remain in a familiar crate lost out on this and threw away a valuable opportunity. The teachers may have seemed crazy at times, be it the Korean Miss Lee dragging meditating children around her classroom by their feet so that they formed orderly lines before showering them with kisses and hugs and sending them on their way, or Mr. Catanzaro, a brilliant social studies teacher, drunk in the boot of our car, peering over the back seat to warn our children that their lives would not be worth living if they mentioned this to anyone on Monday morning. Be it Edward's teacher who had swum with sharks and wrestled crocodiles before pursuing the slightly more sedate post of an international teacher or the music teacher who waddled into a science exam on her hands and knees, palms outstretched bearing a muffin and banana to beg for forgiveness from the science teacher for a previous altercation, they all added to the richness of the school community. America lacked this richness. It was on the whole, although thankfully with some notable exceptions, bland. Bland teachers who had fallen into the profession because they had nowhere else to go, or excellent teachers who had had the life squeezed from their veins by a need to follow a bland curriculum with bland expectations. International schools were never bland. They were the tropical fruit basket of schools and hence the existence of a few unusual nuts amongst their number.

This colour and diversity meant that Mr. Simmons was not the only nudity that was very much part of school life. Mixed-sex showers and progressive school trips were also a surprising discovery. During week without walls the children, from eleven to eighteen years old, were taken on trips to widen their horizons and allow them to push the barriers towards independence. Some parents were not comfortable with their offspring gaining independence and there was an option for them to stay at home, but each day attend a Frankfurt based activity. Again these tended to be American families who were not accustomed to overnight trips until 8th grade and even then only with a year of meetings preceding it and with strict supervision at all times.

The Germans had not fully appreciated the mindset of the kind of parent who chooses to keep their kids at home during a week to promote independence. They had not considered that these families may be generally more conservative. The agenda for the week was generally vague. Monday river trip and group cooked lunch, Tuesday museum, Wednesday art facility, Thursday local community projects, Friday Frankfurt Sports. The week started well with parents reporting a great time had by all cooking pizzas from scratch in the home of one of the Australian teachers in the centre of the city and a trip to the German Film Museum. They were less impressed at the array of sexual acts in the 3D art museum that their eleven to seventeen year olds were exposed to, but now were a little more understanding of my amusement when Henry's Kindergarten class had visited earlier in the year. Still, complaints were lodged, as they should have been made aware of the type of art their innocent little darlings would be exposed to and it was pointed out that the school should have known better following the kindergarten trip. The school was confused. If nudity is not your taboo then this is just a great place for a school trip. Thursday came and it was community project day. American parents looked forward to their children giving back to the community, may be planting a flower bed with bright petunias at the senior centre or helping out at a school giving them a chance to practise their German. They had not expected a whole new set of vocabulary words that they would learn as they visited a local brothel and were taught about safe sex and sexually transmitted diseases by the prostitutes. This was followed by a light lunch in the red light district, before moving on to the needle exchange and drug rehabilitation centre where they would have the opportunity to interview recovering drug addicts as to the circumstances that led them to turn to drugs and the horrors which brought them to rehab. The click, click, click of heavily hit keys on the keyboards of computers around Dreieich could be heard echoing in the still night air that evening and the ping ping ping of the arrival of emails in the principal's inbox the following morning. As in previous years, they would be ignored, safe in the knowledge they would return soon to their homeland and leave things to continue as normal in the Rheinland.

Being the child of a more liberally minded parent, James missed the brothel and needle exchange and opted for a cycling trip around Lake Constance where each day they would cycle a little further along the leafy paths that make up the perimeter of the huge lake bordering Switzerland, Austria and Germany. Even here though the different taboos were evident. He had told a teacher that he wanted to buy beer to take home so he had popped down to the off-license when the teacher went to get their beer. Despite only being thirteen years old, he had come home with a selection of alcoholic beverages. This would have made the national news in America, but in Germany helping kids to buy alcohol to take home was all part of the education process that teachers were there to help with.

My children were not particularly sheltered. I had always believed my job as a parent was not to protect them from the world, but prepare them for it. As James later said he was glad I had parented with "aggressive neglect". By this he meant I allowed them to make mistakes, but held them accountable. Not all children at the school had been furnished with such life skills. One of the girls who did the cycling trip was the daughter of the Pakistani ambassador and spent her life being driven around in a chauffeur driven limo. As a result, she had never really had the need to learn to ride a bike which was to pose quite a problem on a week's cycling holiday around Lake Constance. The teachers taught her how to ride a bike and how to catch a bus and soon she would either, meet up with her classmates for lunch by finding her way to a restaurant on route by bus or, as her cycling skills improved, she would cycle along with them. Her parents were open to the idea of her experiencing new things and as a result, she learnt to be more resourceful and would probably have been safer long term when she finally went to university or spread her wings.

A few months after arriving in Germany, the twelve year old James also learnt a few survival skills when he took part in a Model United Nations trip to the Polish

Parliament building. The trip was really designed for the older kids, maybe fifteen to eighteen, but James was a gifted debater with a love of politics, so had joined a club that did not normally attract younger students. His mature attitude and height had not alerted the teacher to his lack of years and he seemed to be given the same freedoms to wander the city as the older students. James is not an explorer or a rule breaker so played it safe and got his dinner close to the hotel with another boy who was fourteen or fifteen, whilst the older students hit the clubs and pubs of Warsaw. On the first or second night, the group was returning from a late night session of debating and James was playing in the snow as they waited for the bus. In his delight at building a snow sculpture he totally missed the fact that everyone else had gotten on the bus or that the bus had driven off along the streets of Warsaw heading for the hotel and leaving him behind.

It was only as the bus was halfway back to the hotel that the teacher noticed James had not got on, by which time it was too late and anyhow this was a public bus with a set route who would not just go back and find a kid playing in the snow. For James, there was no rubric to follow in this situation, but we had brought him up to figure things out, to think on his feet. The school had the same expectations and had already placed him in situations where he needed to think creatively. Therefore, despite speaking no Polish, and probably having very little money he somehow managed to find another bus and made his way back. He had taken one more step in becoming prepared for the big wide world.

I was less on board with the younger boys being prepared for real life. The school had already lost four year old Henry, who was found wandering the multi-story carpark next to the school. They were unperturbed and felt it was his responsibility to follow the rules and not leave the school without a teacher or parent. This was not a compromise I was willing to take and eventually the school changed their dismissal procedure to ensure children were not just passed to any local pedophile or kidnapper or left to roam the streets. This attitude brought with it an anxiety I was going to have to overcome if we were to make the most of our life here, but I had been subject to the fears of American life for too long. Overnight school trips which were now the norm from a young age would have horrified the parents back in Southborough. Many went into a state of panic over their 8th grader going off to Washington DC for a couple of nights with, air-conditioned coaches taking them wherever they needed to go and shielding them for the horrors of the city. Now I was being asked to send my nine year old off into the much more dangerous hustle and bustle of Berlin where they would ride public transport and be absorbed into the sights, sounds and smells of a cosmopolitan city. Despite the school already having lost two of my children, I sent him, but the teacher knew I was nervous and sent back daily updates and proof of life photos.

Part of the trip was to visit the restaurant owned by a parent at the school who ran exclusive pop up eating establishments all over Europe. Edward tells me it was like walking into a retro antique shop, in which there was a large table and a bus. He said there was art on the walls and a room that they were not allowed to go into with a rude statue of Mickey Mouse. The owner had invited the group to his restaurant before it opened in the evening for an early dinner and to no doubt show off to the chaperoning parents and teachers. His son, Sebastian, was very excited to see his dad, who it seemed spent very little time at home. The boy was compensated for the lack of time he spent with his father with iPhones, iPads, widescreen TVs and every gaming system known to man. His room was a technological palace, every 4th grader's dream. Edward had often noted how he was not as lucky as the kids in his class who had the latest iPhone sandwiched between their reading book and homework in their superhero emblazoned backpacks. My kids had lego and action figures and they were not totally last century as they also had a Wii in the basement which they shared, but apparently not one each in their bedrooms. Sebastian's big moment arrived when he could show all of his class the amazing world his father had created. He and his dad would wow the other nine and ten year olds with this exclusive sold out culinary spectacular. He rushed in to hug his dad who gave him a quick squeeze before pushing him aside, eager to impress the other adults. When he was sure that word would get back to Frankfurt of his success he disappeared without so much as a goodbye to his son. Suddenly, Edward realised that the riches Sebastian had were nothing in comparison to the so far unappreciated riches he had. His life was rich in hugs, rich in love, rich in time together. When he returned home he said he was glad he didn't have an iPhone, but that he did have parents who loved him and wanted to spend time with him. It seemed like a lot for a small boy, but I was so proud of him for realising the value of what we had. He went on to go on trips dog sledding on an alpine glacier, abseiling off enormous cliffs, hanging out at water parks and dancing all night at the disco to celebrate the end of PYP. It certainly beats a couple of soggy sandwiches and a bag of crisps at Chester Zoo which was the highlight of my last year at primary school!

Education was the compromise I was not prepared to make. In our attempts to find our place in the world we all have things we will change and things we need to hold on to as fundamentally what makes us "us". My father had left school at fourteen and came from a home where there was not always the money to pay for his basic needs. He had seen the benefits of education to move himself up into the middle classes and to settle into a comfortable life, unobtainable to his ancestors. This appreciation of hard work and education had been passed down to me. It was ingrained into my being that I was lucky to have the chances I had been given and must grab them with both hands using knowledge and reasoning to pull myself yet further up the ladder away from poverty. I had never wanted for anything. I had clothes, food, heat all the basics and on top of that, I had an endless supply of books and shoes, the two things denied to my father in his younger days. Now my children had even more than I had. They mixed with people whose visions were far from their own who could provide nourishment for their minds from distant lands. I could not understand the unwillingness of American parents to allow their children to open their minds to new ideas instead of opting for brainwashing and propaganda, which they were taught not to question. From the very first day of preschool children were forced to recite the pledge of allegiance every morning until its words were imprinted on their developing brains. They did not need to understand the significance of its words just to believe it was an essential part of being a "True American." When my boys refused to say the pledge of allegiance, preferring to stand in respectful silence, they were rebuked for being disrespectful. Even when they explained that they had two countries and had allegiance to neither one nor the other, as a parent would not choose allegiance to one child or another, they were still berated for their decision to not choose the land that was neither of their birth nor their ancestry. They were not praised for understanding, critically analysing and finally coming to a well formed decision over whether or not to recite the words. Instead they were chastised for failing to bow to propaganda. My children must question. My children must not blindly accept. My children must develop critical thinking skills. My children must be mindful of the world that existed beyond their own and be respectful of it, learn from it. These were my non-negotiables.

8 BEGINNING TO TICK THE BUCKET!

Travel was a form of education that my children were lucky enough to receive. In my attempt to open the boys' eyes to a world beyond their own, Edward wrote a European bucket list of all the things we would do during our time there. It became a mission to tick as many things off that bucket list as we could. Our adventures were not limited to the bucket list however, but it did mean we did not miss any of the highlights and gave purpose to our travel plans. For example, as James asked, "So who are we going to Wank with", I not only realised that some holiday destinations really should have an alternative name, but also that going to Wank may not have been my first thought for a bucket list. We had a limited amount of time in Europe. The whole ex-pat deal with a free car and petrol was not forever, so we tried to cram every spare minute with an adventure.

We went to Prague where we ate meringues as big as our heads and discovered that if you fell off a Segway it just keeps going. The guy walking in front of us also discovered that the hard way about the same time as his legs disappeared from under him and he was pinned to the ground by a runaway Segway being chased by Edward!

We ate black forest gateaux in the Black Forest, well actually we had three separate slices in three separate cafes before we decided we definitely did not like it! We saw the two clocks claiming to be the world's largest cuckoo clocks and visited the workshop of fifth generation young clockmaker, Christophe Herr, in Schonach. Here we helped to design our very own cuckoo clock incorporating his modern take on the traditional hunting clock. We watched as his chisel cut into the softwood to reveal leaves and flowers intertwined in the same way his forefathers' chisels had carved stags and antlers. We stayed in a beautiful hotel in the Black Forest with a romantic restaurant and amazing spa facilities. We all headed for the spa for the afternoon, but Dominic soon discovered that like much of Germany you were expected to be naked in the saunas. He sat down on his towel in his trunks, but was soon asked to leave by the men and women sitting stark naked in rows around the edge of the wooden oasis. Apparently, fabric in the sauna was a taboo, unclean and unhygienic, unlike bare bums pressed against the pine slats which were totally acceptable. Who knew where his swim shorts had been before he had entered the steamy room full of sweaty, naked butt cheeks pressed up against the baking hot wood! As we sat in the restaurant eating a very expensive meal later that night, Dominic informed me that he had, "Seen hers!" "Seen hers!" and wish he hadn't "seen his!" The restaurant was so expensive that the boys were up in the room with Matilda eating pizza so that Dominic could have a date night. Course after course was brought out, each more delightful than the last, until we felt like our stomachs would burst. Apparently, we had been away far too long for Matilda who decided to sneak out and try and find us. As she wandered the corridors it was soon announced in the restaurant that a very big, hairy, black bear was prowling the hotel corridors!

Next, we headed for Paris where we waved at people from the top of the Eiffel Tower and on the way home stopped in Luxembourg to tick another country off our list. During a ludicrously expensive dinner, we all thought of an adjective to describe Luxembourg. We had cold, expensive and shut and then Henry declared that it was "shitty!" Matilda had held it all in, in Paris, as she will only poo and wee on grass. The wee had dribbled out as she walked, but the poo was all saved for the grassy banks of Luxembourg where she provided us with a three-bagger! Not to be left out, Henry suddenly declared he was desperate for the toilet and just could not wait. I looked around and, although there were no toilets to be seen, there was also not a sign of another person. I told him to go quickly in an ornamental flower bed, thinking that he would be able to have a quick wee before anyone arrived. Unfortunately, he had diarrhoea and by the time he had squatted down in the snapdragons and wiped his bum on a hydrangea, there was nothing more to be done than make a very quick exit. I would like to say this was not a typical day in the our family, but, as James was later to point out on the beautiful Corney Fell in the English Lake District, "Henry has defecated on every beautiful landscape I have ever tried to appreciate!"

We stayed in wonderful chateaus, fancy hotels, Travelodges and total dives. Indeed, Dominic did not cope well in an Ibis Budget in Brugge! He became too accustomed to his hotel rooms on business trips to India which had a butler button, so the Ibis's complete lack of soft furnishings and smell of disinfectant made it feel more like he should have a button to call for a nurse!

The nearest I ever got to a butler button was yelling "James" at the top of my voice and then hoping my every whim was catered for as long as I agreed to extend his electronics time. Once I was sat looking at a mountain of laundry waiting to be folded, when Dominic's view of

Mount Fuji, from his hotel window, popped up on my Facebook feed and this simile became a manifestation of our differing lives. All this did, however, mean that my expectations of the hotel life were so much lower. Sometimes we got lucky with an upgrade like when we had a suite in Poole in Dorset with a big old fashioned bath in the living room. I ordered room service and laid in the hot soapy water whilst eating the smoked salmon sandwiches and watching Restoration Home with surround sound. On other trips, we were less lucky. The words you just don't want to hear when you arrive at your Dutch hotel, to tick off, "Seeing the Tulips of Amsterdam" from the bucket list, are "Oh we upgraded you to luxury room, but didn't realise you had children so we will have to change you back to a family room!" Edward consoled himself with the two cherry liqueur chocolates off his pillow and then informed us that he would regret it in the morning because he would not be able to cope with the hangover!

Trips to Italy were evenly spaced throughout our three years. Our first stop was fairly early in our time in Europe when I hadn't realised that shouting to be understood was not the best way forward, but maybe that was for the best because sometimes people are rude and it's not a cultural thing, they are just rude! Dominic was away with work so we made the trip to Rome alone, knowing he would join us the following day. I had booked a hotel close to the colosseum so we were right in the middle of things. When the taxi pulled up outside we really were right in the middle of things. Despite it being about 11 o'clock at night, the streets were full of people. Dancing and singing, they jostled on the crowded cobbles for a little bit of space to call their own. We fought our way with our cases across the tiny uneven pavement to the hotel door and eventually to the safety of the lobby. I gave our name and explained that we had a family suite booked for the next few nights. You can imagine my surprise when a huge metal key, which hung from a blue tassel, and a map were thrust in my hand

and I was directed back into the thronging mass of people that filled the streets outside to find my room. The taxi was long gone and the man told me that our room was down the street outside through the masses of inebriated party goers and up a side street. I had been frightened that the children would be swept up in the wave of frivolity and debauchery on the short trip across the pavement from the taxi, but I was assured it was not far and I would be fine. I instructed each of them to hold on to the suitcase of their neighbour as we congaed down the street slithering between the crowds. As I reached a door that seemed correct on the map, I tried to insert the key, but with no luck. I tried any neighbouring doors that may have been a possibility and then checked the map again as a wave of despair came over me. The realisation I would have to fight my way back to the hotel for help filled me with terror. It had taken us maybe ten to fifteen minutes to get here and now I was going to have to repeat the whole process in reverse.

We eventually completed the terrifying and exhausting walk back to the hotel and I asked the man to help me to find the room. Despite him sitting and reading his paper and smoking a cigarette, when we had walked in both times, he informed us he was far too busy and we would need to find it on our own. This was not going to happen. I was given no additional instruction, nothing that would make a second attempt any more likely to be successful than the first. I explained that I had tried really hard and that I did not feel safe trying again, but he became quite aggressive and told me I must try alone. I had become far too German to take this sort of behaviour and since a "Das geht nicht" was not an option, I told him that we would sleep on the floor of the lobby. We all laid down by his desk and rested our heads on the suitcases. This was not what he had anticipated and after a moment of shocked disbelief, he became more and more irate and shouted that we were blocking the lobby and we could not sleep there. I informed him we were. He shouted. I remained steadfast. He shouted some more. He informed me he would call the Police. I asked if they knew where my room was and would help me. He locked up put a note on the door and walked me to a side street that bore little relation to where was marked on the map. I slammed the heavy door behind me as I informed him that no real man would ever treat a woman and children like he had just done, and that in England men were real men. My real English man arrived the next day and the fighting continued at Gladiator School where the boys were dressed in red togas and taught to fight with wooden swords by a man in an equally small red toga. We soon discovered that the chaos of the previous night had been a festival that lasted into the next day, but now it was not as frightening. The streets were familiar, I was not encumbered by heavy baggage and we were together. This was almost a metaphor for life as a trailing spouse. As things become familiar, you are not encumbered by needless baggage and as long as you have each other to lean on life doesn't seem so scary and you see the laughter and joy. That night though I seemed to be the only member of my family who saw the laughter and joy and wanted to stay up all night dancing in the street and eating macaroons. We partook in the celebrations for a little while to keep me happy and then went back to the apartment for an early night.

On the last night, we asked some locals we met in a pizza shop where they would go to eat and they advised us to cross the river to an area well known for restaurants. We had seen Rome as tourists, but not seen Rome as a Roman. We had eaten our pasta to tick off eat Pasta in Rome, visited the Colosseum and the ruins next to it, went to the Trevi fountain and the Spanish Steps and then to the Vatican. The whole of Rome consumed in three days! Edward seemed to take to the idea of one day becoming Pope and informed us that as Pope what you say goes, you get to wear a cool outfit and best of all you get a bobblehead that looks like you! It was difficult to argue with him without going into the whole celibacy thing so we accepted that, as a self-confessed atheist, this may not be his best career choice, but you need to let them choose their own path. As we crossed the river away from the bobbleheads and fake centurions we entered a different world. It was beautiful and not touristy at all. The streets were filled with couples in love walking arm and arm down half empty streets, blissfully staring into each other's eyes unaware of a world beyond their lover's gaze. Restaurants lined the streets interspersed by independent grocery stores, their wares piled up outside. A handcrafted jewellery shop or artist studio were the only purveyors of non edible produce and signified that trade was aimed at the local market. The food was amazing and a fraction of the price of the other side of the river. We sat and soaked up the atmosphere, Italian voices overwhelmingly loud, yet a comforting lack of English being spoken. A great way to finish our time there.

Venice was also a sublimely magnificent place like no other. I had imagined it to be crowded and full of tourists, another Disney like tourist trap of plastic gondoliers and cheap prints, but it wasn't. I think the fact that we went in October really helped. Although global warming is a real problem for the sinking city, the unseasonably warm weather was a blessing for us. The sky was bright blue as we boarded the water taxi and once again I was swept back in time to feel like a Victorian lady on a grand tour. Dominic suddenly saw the romance in the whole situation and we sat holding hands outside Caffè Florian in St. Mark's Square having afternoon tea and watching the world go by. It was as though time was still for us, but racing by for everyone else. We went on a gondola and were serenaded by a man with an accordion and just wandered the streets looking in the shops and soaking up the atmosphere.

Travel soon became the norm for us, at times even a chore. When Edward informed us that he just goes on holiday, eats the local specialist food, buys a snow globe and then its job done, I realised that this jet setting life had really become the unexceptional to them. Back home in Massachusetts most of the people we knew were born there, holidayed on the Cape, and would die there. A trip to Vermont was almost considered going abroad! For my children being in a different country every weekend was what everybody did. It wasn't a great opportunity anymore or an adventure it was just normality. Indeed Henry told us "It doesn't matter if I get lost I would just find a policeman and tell him I live in a Travelodge." I wanted them to appreciate what we had, to see that everyone wasn't existing in a tropical fruit basket like ours, and that they were lucky to have ventured beyond a plastic crate of identical fruits, but our basket almost became their crate. It was their mainstream, their normal.

As we entered our third year to my surprise all the travel and adventures were becoming a drudgery for the kids and maybe even for Dominic, but never for me. Although at times I almost needed a holiday to recover from booking all the holidays. When you've seen the Alps you have seen all mountains. When you have seen Paris and Rome you have seen all cities. When you have felt the crunch of Belgium waffles in Brugge and tasted the rich chocolate sauce as it glides down your throat or smelt the heady perfume as you bite into Rose Turkish Delight in Istanbul or the sharp vinegar of British fish and chips sat on a stone wall with the bracing Pennine breeze penetrating every tiny gap in your clothing, there is no food that will ever tickle your taste buds in the same way. You have done it all, seen it all, smelt it all and tasted it all. What is left to be imagined? With the education of travel comes the normalisation of the exotic, the unknown.

When I woke Dominic up at 7 am to head to Neuschwannstein castle I shouted, "Come on its going to be so exciting. We are going to see the castle the Disney castle is based on." His reply as he rolled over and attempted to go back to sleep was, "Why would I want to do that when I've seen the real Disney castle." On the way home I was not feeling very romantic driving the Romantiacher Road with three kids, the smelliest dog north of the alps and a husband who told me he was wishing he was playing golf! The unknown was normalised and mundane. It had lost its magic.

In the July before we left, I dragged three reluctant boys to Florence for our final Italian Adventure. They were really not that keen to go, but I knew that we would not have all these opportunities again. We needed to tick off the leaning tower from the bucket list and I had seen pictures of Cinque Terra, a series of five fishing villages, only accessible by boat, with multi-coloured houses rising up from sheltered coves. I wanted to see it. I wanted to see Sienna. I did not want to miss a thing. Dominic had often mentioned how beautiful it was, so we ordered a car to pick us up from our apartment in the centre of Florence early in the morning and take us out for the day. Sienna was a little disappointing to me, but it had the most wonderful handbag shop I had ever seen. I am not a handbag kind of a girl, but I saw a beautiful blue leather bag embossed with leaves and flowers. It obviously was wonderful because for years to come I would receive so many compliments on it. There was one problem. As they regularly did, Bank of America had stopped my credit card because they suspected fraudulent use. Apparently, my card had been used in Germany, no kidding I live there! Anyway, this meant I only had the cash in my purse. There was just enough to buy the bag with nothing left over. Nothing if the kids got thirsty and needed a drink. Nothing for an ice cream. Just enough for the bag. As I am sure you have already realised the bag won over the kids' needs for water and sugar.

We set off to a place the driver had arranged lunch for us and the car wound up hillsides covered in olive groves and vineyards in the Tuscan countryside until we eventually arrived at an old farmhouse. I was suspicious as we ventured into the middle of nowhere and wondered if the driver was a friend of the farmer and was bringing some gullible tourists to be ripped off, but I went with the flow. They made their own cheese and wine and under a vine covered veranda were two long picnic tables we sat to eat lunch. There was no choice of food and the lady brought dishes of sliced tomatoes and basil, plates of cheese and olives and a basket of crusty bread cut into chunks. There was water, peach juice or wine to drink and we all tucked into the food placed in front of us. Dominic had not come on this trip with us and never have I wanted him to experience something more than I did there. Whenever we went away he always loved to get bread and cheese and some local tomatoes. To him, it was the taste of being on holiday. I used to laugh at him getting so excited about a cheese and tomato sandwich, but he loved it, really really loved it. For the first time, I understood what he meant. This was the best food I had ever tasted. The tomatoes, fresh off the vine were full of flavour and the cheese had a saltiness that complimented their sweetness perfectly. This was as simple as a meal could be, but also as perfect as any meal could be. This was a taste that would never come from an American supermarket, a taste you had to be on a Tuscan hillside to truly appreciate.

After we had eaten, the farmer's wife showed us how they made the cheese and the wine and then the boys sat on a stone wall overlooking the valley with their sketchbooks and painted what they saw. Sitting in the farm and having lunch and admiring the view was to become one of my favourite things I had done in all the time we were living in Germany. It was such a simple day again. A day to be thankful for what I had, for the chances that the past three years had given us. A time for quiet contemplation with my boys. A precious time.

The holiday had the perfect ending when somehow we ended up in business class for the flight home from Florence. Henry wanted a window seat so I told him to move to the row behind me "That won't make me lower class will it?" he said. "No sweetheart! Swinging an upgrade means you were always lower class just lucky! Luckier than you truly appreciate at this moment"

9 ESCAPE FROM THE SLOVENIAN GESTAPO!

Whenever Edward was asked to play two truths and a lie, it always included the time we got arrested in Slovenia. In fairness to me, I was only there in an attempt to calm him down after his stressful skiing incident where the whole of an intermediate ski class had a near-death experience. It wasn't my fault that his anxiety soared as he watched his mother being bundled into a police van. His dad was never held responsible despite being no help and the excuse of being smeared all over in chocolate by a busty Austrian did not seem a reasonable excuse to me. Anyway, maybe I should start at the very beginning, a very good place to start so Julie Andrews tells me!

Edward's Bucket List meant crazy trips became par for the course. I had my own little list and I was desperate to run down the mountain in Salzburg to recreate the opening scene in the Sound of Music.

The hotel had appeared to be an amazing spa hotel, but it felt more like an anorexics retreat. Weighing scales in our hotel room, the hotel being used to film Germany's Next

Top Model and when my dessert came it was huge then they poured over a little jug of orange stuff and it revealed it was not huge, but a tiny dessert hiding under a big chocolate dome which melted away. I was supposed to be impressed, but shrinking my dessert was never going to impress me so we headed into Salzburg for the rest of our meals. A day was spent in Hitler's mountain retreat, his nest. Another was spent in a salt mine where we headed into the depths of an Austrian hillside on a giant slide closely followed by German pensioners all wearing boiler suits who looked like retired Oompa Loompas and seemed to have a joy of life which could only be envied. Eventually, after many evenings watching the film, came the day of the sound of Music tour. We headed off on a bus, the sound of Julie Andrews blaring out of the speakers, visiting all the locations from the film where me and the boys, well mainly me and Edward, recreated the songs from, "I am 16 going on seventeen" in the summer house to, "The Cuckoo Song" on the back seat of the bus.

When I say we visited all the locations there was one screaming omission. Where was the mountain? With a little help from google, we found its location and headed for the town, but there was no sign pointing us to the top of the mountain where Maria had twirled, grey skirt swinging in the alpine breeze as the music crescendoed from bird song to a rousing "The Hills are Alive". We asked two ladies out walking, but they had no idea what we were talking about. Next, we asked in the village shop and at last someone who knew where we were looking for. She directed us up a lane on the outskirts of the village and eventually after a succession of turns and little roads we found the field. That was all it was, a field. Not some major tourist attraction just a field in front of a farm where a man was sat on his tractor. That was not going to stop me. I quickly stripped down to my underwear and loaded myself into my dirndl, nudity was no taboo to me anymore! Then arms outstretched, I ran out into the field, spinning around, arms still stretching wide as the mountain view belting out "the hills are alive with the sound of music". After a short run across the hillside, I jumped back in the car and we drove off leaving a bemused tractor driver wondering if he had been working so hard he had started to hallucinate! That however, was to be a fairly tame day in the Alpine region compared to what was to follow in our final January in Germany.

We decided this final winter was the time to tick off skiing in the Alps from the bucket list. As the car chugged off down the road, skis strapped to the roof, children squabbling in the back about who had the middle seat, we had no idea of the dangers which lay ahead. We drove and drove until the grassy banks beside the road became whiter and whiter. As we crossed the Austrian border, we saw the mountains rising up ahead of us. Forests of fir trees glistening with snow rose up from the sides of the winding roads towards the top of the snow covered rocky summits. It looked like a Christmas card. We got closer and closer to Bad Kleinkirchheim and the beautiful spa hotel we had booked, but we were all getting more and more tired.

We were glad to find the hotel and wander towards the reception area where a big log fire was burning. We soon discovered that the little town was the location for the Women's World Cup Downhill Championships. The boys had not skied much since leaving America and Henry had still to perfect his skills so we booked everyone lessons on a small slope next to the hotel. They soon began to find their ski legs and within a couple of days, James and Edward had moved up to a fairly advanced group. Dominic was getting a little achy and was struggling to find boots that really worked for him so he decided to spend the day in the hotel spa. I took the boys over to the slope. Henry had his lesson on the same slope they had been practising on the previous couple of days, but the older boys group soon set off to the larger mountain. Henry hurtled down the little slope on his final run whooping with joy at his newfound confidence. Dominic had failed to get an appointment in the spa, so had booked one for the following day and had now joined Henry and I in the little cafe at the bottom of the smaller slope to wait for the older boys to return. We sipped on our hot chocolate and waited. We ordered a second drink and a sandwich and we waited. We watched people come and go, fall over and get back up and we waited, but there was no sign of James and Edward's class. Eventually, we asked where they were and were told that sometimes they could have taken a different turn or may have less experienced skiers so they may go a little longer. Time continued to pass and still no sign. They were now over an hour late and I was starting to worry when from around a tree the instructor appeared, face as white as the snow beneath his skis, followed by his trembling pupils whose skin seemed to vary from grey to green, but none with the red rosy glow of a fun day on the slopes.

"Is it OK if I don't do my lesson tomorrow?" Edward pleaded after the instructor had explained why they were so late. Apparently, they had taken a wrong turn and ended up on the women's downhill World Championship course during their practice run. The course had been lovingly prepared to be a sheet of ice, which at times had almost vertical drops. Once on the course, the group was unable to return and had no choice, but to complete it. Linsey Vonn the Women's world champion may have done the course in under two minutes, but my boys made it down in under 35. I doubted Linsey was quite so traumatised!

The next day Henry had a ski lesson and James just wanted to stay in the hotel and maybe regain his confidence on the bunny slopes. Dominic had booked a chocolate massage in the hotel spa which he had no intention of missing, but Edward on the other hand was so traumatised that he did not want to even see a pair of skis. I had the wonderful idea of adding a new country to his bucket list.

Dominic had recently been to Ljubljana the capital of Slovenia and had said what a beautiful city it was, rich in history and culture, so Edward decided to add, "find some culture in Slovenia" to his bucket list. We woke early and set off towards the border. It was a lovely sunny day with blue skies and seemed the perfect day for a bit of quality mother and son time. We turned on the radio and sang along to the songs as we crossed the border into Slovenia and headed to Ljubljana.

When we got there we parked the car and went to see what the city had to offer. We struggled to find much to do considering it was a capital city, but explored a couple of museums and made the most of the coffee shops and ice cream parlours. As the rickety monorail pulled us up to the castle it was evident that Slovenia was a country that was only starting to develop a tourist industry. I wasn't sure if we would make it to the top, but eventually, the car pulled into the docking area and we got out to discover the ruins of a castle high on a hill, overlooking the city. Edward found a foam sword in the gift shop and fought a selection of invisible advisories with all the energy you would need to fight for your life in any medieval war. When every last invisible soldier had been defeated we headed to the monorail and cranked down the hill to the bottom. After buying the obligatory Christmas decoration for our tree we headed back to the car and began the long journey back to the hotel to hear of everyone's adventures which we hoped were a little less eventful than the previous day.

As we approached the border we were pulled over by a man in a blue uniform and I was asked to get out of the car. He spoke to me only in German and I asked if he could speak English, but he just scowled and continued to talk German. I told him I was worried about leaving Edward in the car alone, but he insisted and told me to get my passport and documents before walking me towards a police van. He bundled me into the back and I sat on a hard bench that ran along the sidewall. At the end backing on to the driver's area was a table with a computer and printer. He told me that I had not purchased a sticker that allowed me to drive in Slovenia when I had entered the country earlier that day, and that I must now buy the sticker and pay a fine which would be a total of 500 Euros in cash. I explained that I did not have that kind of money in cash, but could pay by credit card, but he was insistent that I pay in cash and became a little more aggressive. "I didn't have cash," I told him again, but he did not seem to believe me and started to shout that I must pay the fine or go to prison. I was very frightened and told him again that I only had a credit card to which he told me he would drive me to a cashpoint. I explained that my young son was in the car and I did not want to leave him, but he refused to take Edward with us. Something did not feel right and I did not want to leave Edward. I definitely did not want to go with a man who was shouting at me to God knows where. He became more and more aggressive. I became more and more frightened, but I stood my ground, being more frightened of what would happen if I carried out his wishes than resisted. This went on for what seemed like forever, but was probably only about 20 or 25 minutes.

Salvation arrived in the form of another policeman. I asked him if Edward was ok, since he had been sitting alone on the hard shoulder for nearly half an hour. I tried to look strong and hid my fear the best I could, but I was worried for my child like any mother would be. The other policeman asked if I did not have a credit card to pay the 100 Euro fine and suddenly I realised that his colleague was not all he seemed, but instead was a corrupt swindler trying to get 400 Euros by terrifying a helpless mother who just wanted to return to the relative safety of a ski resort where her son had been scared half to death the day before. My credit card was swiped and I escaped his clutches. I immediately rang Dominic, still shaking, to tell him what had happened, but there was no reply. His phone just vibrated on the bedside table in our room as he was rubbed all over by a busty blonde holding a big tub of cocoa solids. A couple of days later we set off home with an Austrian style chair in the boot to await the arrival of a cabinet painted with Austrian scenes. As Dominic asked why we could not just pick up a traditional souvenir rather than a selection of items to redesign our living room, I reminded him that he had almost not had a wife or children to adorn his home so should be grateful for what we were bringing home!

10 A LIFE AS INTERNATIONAL WEAPONS SMUGGLERS

Worrying about weapons often accompanied our trips. Although little worry accompanied the separate bag of weapons we often packed just because we were travelling with boys who needed a foam or wooden sword to keep them occupied as they travelled around concurring Europe. Leaving Istanbul was a different matter though when Dominic almost reenacted a scene from Midnight Express. Our trip there was full of unexpected obstacles though so it came as no surprise that Dominic was nearly up close and personal with a Turkish guard's rubber gloves!

It all started well enough. Dominic was on a business trip to Istanbul staying in an amazing hotel, top of the range luxury. He had shown us pictures of the all you could eat Turkish delight trolleys in every corridor so we would have no problem ticking off "Eat Turkish Delight in Turkey" from the Bucket List. Even the airport was easy. Apparently travelling with three boys counted as a major disability and I was rushed through the empty line for disabled people as we arrived at the Flughafen to join Dominic at the end of his trip. Even the teddy bears got boarding passes. Henry had a sore thumb, but we had checked it out with the doctor at 7 am that morning and he had given us some antibiotics just in case because we were travelling so far. He had popped the tiny white blister of puss next to his nail and added a little antiseptic for good measure. Now we were excited to be on our way and were getting ready to board. I glanced at his thumb as the ground crew started to open the gate and noticed that there was a red line coming from his thumb and heading towards his elbow. I rang the doctor to check this was ok and he told me on no account must I board the plane, but must get him to the hospital as soon as possible. I told the airline staff who said to wait until they had boarded the plane and then they would help me by showing me the first aid in the airport. The doctor had told me that if the red line reached his armpit the infection would reach his bloodstream and this could be fatal. As the line was already an inch further up his arm, I had no intention of waiting to be checked out by a first aider after a plane full of passengers had loaded. I set off back the way I had come, but hadn't realised that it was very rare for people to leave an airport on foot rather than on a plane and airports just are not set up to easily leave.

Eventually, we made it to the car and after speeding past a couple of speed cameras I checked into the emergency room. I explained how my child was close to death in my very best German and the lady wrote "infected thumb" on the sheet and told me to wait. I explained the urgency and was told, "Warten" in that low steady slow voice people use for the deaf, foreigners and idiots. This was accompanied by a lot of pointing, so I sat and rang the doctor who had seen him that morning so he could explain. Despite her taking the phone from me and there being a lot of "Yah Yah Yah" I was told again to "War... ten..." I had rung my friend Laurie on my way to the hospital to come and get the other boys and when she arrived, despite speaking good German, we were still told to "warten." The red line was now past his elbow so I grabbed him by the hand and rushed through the double doors to where I knew the doctors were, with the lady on the desk yelling at me as I disappeared from view. She ran from her position, but it was too late, the doctor had seen the line and was rushing us into a cubicle to put Henry on IV antibiotics. Soon we were checked into a room with a little girl and her dad. They were very nice, but like the nurses spoke no English. It was all very frightening.

Even when people understand you as a foreigner they assume that you are not saying what you meant to say so they believe their own assumptions are correct. Being an immigrant translates into most people's minds as having a low IQ. You feel vulnerable and scared. An adventure is one thing, learning about other cultures and other ways to think, but when that may mean you cease to exist because your words become worthless, you wonder if you made the right decision. I was not fleeing persecution like many of the people on my German language course, I was just fleeing boredom. This altered the scales for risk and benefit. For the man on my course who had been a lawyer in Afghanistan helping the allied forces, when the lives of his family and himself were threatened by the Taliban, it made sense to flee to Germany and risk being treated like a second class citizen by a hospital receptionist whose only day of persecution had been when someone pushed in front of her at the nail salon. The Afghan man attended the class in the morning and worked as a hotel porter all afternoon and evening and grabbed weekend jobs on building sites when he could. He came late to class only once and was rebuked for his lack of commitment, but did not explain that he had been unable to get hold of his mother for five days and was worried if she had been shot on her way to the market, a punishment for his crimes of helping the British and Americans. That morning she had called and he spent a minute too long talking to her and had missed the bus. He ran to class, probably quite a distance, but he would never run as fast as the bus so was a little late. People saw him carry their bags at the hotel, but didn't ask his story. How could a leather skinned porter, invisible in the shadows ever be smart or valued as he milked the system dry, taking nothing and giving everything? He may have been intelligent, well educated and successful in his own language, but with an unfamiliar accent and a couple of grammar mistakes he was consigned to the back of the queue. People of privilege judge others on grammar, on spelling, on accent. They make assumptions, but do not question. They don't value content only convention. They had no reason to judge him, only reason to look inwardly and judge themselves, falling short on so many levels. He had a reason for putting his family through this that benefitted them. He was brave, selfless and commendable. Unlike him, I had done this on a whim. I realised health, like education, was a non-negotiable.

Laurie came back later in the evening and brought us a DVD player and a couple of DVDs one being "Valiant" the story of pigeons talking in fake German accents as they infiltrated the German lines of Nazi carrier pigeons. There were no headphones so not the best choice for a German hospital room. It did cut through a very boring situation where the highlight of the day was dripping jam from my doughnut on my arm and playing tunes by rubbing the rubbery cheese against our teeth. Dominic had flown back when he discovered our predicament and thank god, because Henry was still in the hospital, when Edward was diagnosed with strep throat! Not surprising when we discovered that the infection that had caused all Henry's problems was strep and was the result of him biting his nails. Henry left the hospital on January 25th and we prepared to travel to Morocco three weeks later.

Despite Edward always being a little accident prone, I assumed that he would get through those three weeks without jeopardising yet another holiday. He seemed to survive running into another kid in the playground and bumping heads on the Monday before we flew to Morocco. He even seemed to survive a second hard hit to the head with a rugby ball the very next day, but Edward's third head injury of the week when he tripped and smashed his head against a granite step was just a step too far, so to speak. After a trip to the same doctor who had drained the puss from Henry's finger only three weeks earlier, we were continuing to tick off hospitals from what seemed like a new bucket list of international medical facilities.

The hospital wanted to admit him for observations after so many head injuries in only four days and I wondered if they thought I may have Munchausen's by proxy! There were no free beds in the hospital, however, so the play area had been converted to a ward with four beds squeezed into the tiny space surrounded by boxes of toys and games. Edward's bed was furthest from the door between the wall and another boy who seemed to also being monitored for concussion. Every hour or so the doctor would come in and lift Edward's eyelids, check his pupils and move on the to boy in the next bed. Soon, diagonally across from Edward, next to the door, a girl arrived who was throwing up all over her bedding and then she was joined in the next bed by a girl who seemed to have a fever and slipped in and out of consciousness. The doctor came in to do her checks again and first visited the bed with the vomiting child, then the one with the high fever and then the other suspected concussion. At no point did she wash her hands between patients. Edward was showing no signs of concussion so effectively was a healthy child who had been admitted to hospital. As the professional plague rat headed towards my healthy child I felt the need to defend him and asked her to wash her hands. She was very offended and said there was no need as she had hardly touched the other patients, but I stood my ground. I was getting used to doing that and was now becoming quite proficient. Since there were still no signs of concussion, I decided to discharge him for his own safety and the next day as we sat on the plane to Morocco I was glad that, as yet, our only disaster was that I had forgotten to shave my legs!

Morocco was amazing! We went with friends from the boys' school who had lived there and another family from the school and stayed in a beautiful all-inclusive resort in Marrakech. We would all go into the city and wander around the medina and medieval streets. The sounds and smells assaulted your senses, so different from the European cities which could mould into one. Street vendors cooked in the main square and the smell of all the spices wafted over to you as you passed them. Snake charmers played on flutes, at times competing with the call to prayer blasting out of loudspeakers from the top of the mosque, as their cobras swayed this way and that. In the markets were huge vibrantly coloured sacks of spices, the yellows, greens and golds of the spices themselves contrasting with the magenta and teal hessian sacks. As you passed the stalls the traders would try to tempt you into their shops with promises of high quality goods and great prices. On the first night, we sat on the roof of a restaurant that overlooked the medina drinking mint tea and just people watching, soaking up the atmosphere. Back in Frankfurt some of the American parents had said that they would never visit a "country like that" because they were worried about their safety, but I felt safer than ever there. There was a warmth to the people and an acceptance of others which I had already experienced from the three soft spoken Moroccans on my German course. It seemed to be part of their culture to share their culture and to want others to enjoy the best of their hospitality. America seemed to be full of propaganda that Islamic countries were dangerous and that was not my experience either here or visiting family in Turkey.

Over the next few days, we joined the other families on walking tours using a guide book which took us down the narrow streets which were full of ordinary looking doors. The book told us to venture behind these facades to experience a whole new world hidden from view. As we went through simple doors, pointed out in the guide book, we were led into palaces, gardens and medieval schools all elaborately decorated in azure blue tiles accented with greens, golds and purples and deep cedar and citron wooden fretwork. These building's wealth was not only in their beauty, but also in the calmness they imparted as you entered. There was a quiet that was only interrupted by the sound of water flowing into ornately tiled fountains.

Things were a little less calm when we decided to take a taxi to a different market on the outskirts of the city. As the kids piled in, Marion, the teacher from the school who had lived in Morocco, noticed that there were no seatbelts and that her precious son. Tiberius, could not possibly travel without a seatbelt. She told him to get out of the car and get in the next taxi and then told my boys to get into the car with no seatbelts. When I pointed out that we should find two taxis that had seatbelts for all kids, she told me that there were only two taxis there and that Tiberius was her only child. I think the fact that I had not only an heir, but two spares was supposed to mean that sticking them in a death trap to swerve in and out of the heavy traffic at speed, was statistically a risk worth taking, as the odds meant that at least one of them would probably survive the journey to buy a few trinkets and souvenirs! After having experienced the madness of Marrakech drivers and traffic for the last few days I disagreed and said I would rather have ten minutes less shopping time and get there in one piece. We waited for the next taxi to arrive.

Marion was a fascinating peach who thought she was a kumquat, married to a dragon fruit. She had taught in

Bahrain, Morocco and now Germany and her ambition to reach the top in her profession was only superseded by her protective instinct towards Tiberius Catanzaro, her only child. She knew that this level of helicopter parenting was an issue, but could not help herself and somehow made her quite endearing. Her husband Barry was on the opposite end of the scale. He was a hunting and fishing kind of guy from Montana who Dominic had placed in bed with his bike and who had curled up in a drunken stupor in the boot of our car on more than one occasion. He would encourage Tiberius to jump from the highest diving board, explore every hidden space, and push the boundaries. He taught history effortlessly, but brilliantly inspiring every student who entered his class even the uninspirable. Marion had a hidden stone so big that it almost poked through her dusty, fuzzy, peachy skin. She followed the rules and respected every taboo in an attempt not to jeopardise her path up the career ladder, but she saw herself as the maverick she would never be. Barry on the other hand was that maverick. Pushing boundaries, not caring what others thought, living life to the full. A strange mix for a marriage, but it worked.

Dominic was happy in Morocco with his buddy Barry. There were golf courses to visit and he always loved an all-inclusive so, when the car came to pick up just our family from our luxury hotel to drive for two days over the Atlas mountains to camp in a tent in the Sahara desert, he really did not see the point. The all-wheel-drive was thankfully in possession of all of its seatbelts although it was a little cramped for the five of us. James clambered into the back seat squashed up in the boot amongst the small cases we and the driver had brought to get us through the next few days. As we headed out of the city and eventually caught a glimpse of the Atlas mountains rising up in front of us. At first, there were lush green terraces framed by the more distant beige sandy mountains, some with a white frosting of snow. As we ventured further the landscape became more barren as the greenery melted into the distance. We stopped at cafes for drinks and snacks, but only pausing for a second to stare in wonder at the beauty before us. The more western dress and dust covered cars were replaced by barefoot Berber children and carts pulled by oxen and I again felt like a Victorian explorer venturing into the unknown. We visited a workshop where they produced Argan oil that was only available in that area and apparently had the ability to make you stay young forever. We went to a town clinging to the side of a hill made of mud houses filled with souvenir shops, which apparently had been used in several films. Eventually, we reached our stop for the night where we had dinner and fell asleep dreaming of what the next day may bring.

As we set off the next day, shoehorned into the Jeep, Moroccan music playing from the CD player, we did not realise how soon we would run out of road. As the Jeep hurtled across a dusty area of flat ground, with little more than cactuses as landmarks, I wondered how the driver knew where to go and if we would ever make it out of the barren expanse that greeted us as we had descended the Atlas Mountains. Sure enough we popped out onto a dusty road with buildings that could be considered a town by local standards. Edward was now dressed in a large woollen caftan that he had bought in the market in Marrakech. Always desperate to immerse himself in the local culture, he would eat whatever the locals ate and now seemed to be the first ginger Moroccan!

Each of the boys wore knitted hats we had bought in the market, but only Edward was greeted by the camel herder waiting with our transport for the next part of our journey with, "Hey Mohammed!" The camel herder was also dressed in a long caftan, but unlike Edward's warm brown wool his was made out of Prussian blue cotton that mirrored the colour of the sky reaching down to the sand dunes ahead. He had a white cloth wrapped around his head like Lawrence of Arabia, but unlike the intrepid Lawrence, he had brown trousers and a black T-shirt with modern American slogans peeping out of his blue robe. We each mounted a camel and set off into the desert that stretched endlessly before us. The man led the first camel and the others followed. His leather flip flops sunk deeper into the sand the further we travelled from the road and the Jeep that still had all our cases squeezed into the back. I wondered how long we would need to traverse this amazing landscape to reach our campsite. How would I manage in such a remote location so far from civilisation? There were obviously no trees to disappear behind for a quick wee so how would all that work!?

I was a little disappointed that the camel ride only lasted about half an hour, but the men of the family were quite relieved. A camel's gate is such that they move both their left legs followed by both the right legs, unlike a horse who moves front left, back right then front right, back left. Who would know that this gate coupled with a hard lump at the front of the saddle means that the crown jewels take quite a hammering! My worries about the remoteness of the campsite and toilet facilities were also a little unfounded. My notion of being a victorian adventure exploring the wilderness of the desert was crushed a little as we were shown to our tent. As the guide flicked the light switch, powered by a solar panel behind the campsite, our large wrought iron bed covered in crisp white linens and a heavy tapestry bedspread was fully illuminated. My fears of scorpions crawling over me as I led in the sand, in a tent made of a few poles and a cloth, now seemed a little ridiculous. After being shown the flushing toilets and the tent containing warm showers which were to one side of our Sahara Disney, we met with other people who had ventured from far and wide on the ships of the desert, navigating the dunes to find our hidden Oasis. There was a couple from Norwich who had also taken a Jeep and been met by a guy in flip flops and Lawrence costume, and a couple of backpackers from Scotland who had come on a bus. We were all summoned by a gong into a large tent with low tables and benches padded with heavily woven fabrics which also hung on the walls. We were surrounded by thick cushions also covered in vibrantly coloured woven fabrics and each table was covered in a scarlet tablecloth on which was placed an amazing meal of tagine and other local delicacies. We talked to the other guests, drank mint tea and ate the wonderful food before heading out to the fire in the centre of the ring of tents. Here all the guides who had led the camels into the camp now became musicians playing instruments and singing local folk songs. The moans of the camels to the edge of the camp joined in with the tunes and Edward still in his warm woollen caftan now pulled up his knitted cap to keep his ears warm in the cold desert air, played the drum. There was an enchanting simplicity as we sat there under the pitch black sky bespangled with celestial diamonds. Deep down I knew we were part of a business set up to give tourists a taste of a bygone age of nomadic desert wanders, but it was nice to be away from the hustle and bustle and just appreciate nature, even if it was powering the running water, light switches and other home comforts. The music was simple and the children were immersed in a world not powered by google just by their imaginations. Of course, we all went to bed long before Edward who forced his eyes open to enjoy every last moment of his cultural overload.

The next morning we got up early to climb the dune next to the camp and watched the sunrise. For every three steps forward I climbed I slid back two so unfortunately the sun made it to the top of the dune long before I did. We loaded our bags back into the Jeep which had arrived with our belongings the night before and watched it speed off into the distance as we climbed on our camels to make the same journey in a much slower and less comfortable way.

On the journey home, we had the chance to stretch out our concertinaed bodies from the cramped jeep when we stopped at a shop selling "antiques," most of which I suspect were made the previous week. Here the boys were each given bright blue lengths of fabric and shown how to wrap them around their heads to get the whole Lawrence camel herder effect. Despite his ginger locks being hidden beneath the reams of fabric which now encircled his head and concealed his nose and mouth, Edward's blue eyes and blond lashes peeping through the slit in the azure blue sea of cloth meant that his appearance still did not fully embrace the Moroccan mystique.

When I worked for a company that imported furniture from China and Africa during my school holidays, I had always been fascinated by a type of chair used by nomadic travellers. They consisted of two pieces of elaborately carved wood that slotted together to form a chair, but could be easily unslotted to lie flat for easy transportation. Here in this shop was such a chair. I hadn't seen one now in over 20 years so my chance of ever seeing one again was pretty slim. I knew I had to buy it. Dominic knew that any common sense talk on his part was totally futile when I was this determined, although when we arrived carrying the enormous heavy pieces of wood I think the driver had wished that at least he had tried. Since there was not really room in the jeep to fit all of my children, a few tense minutes followed discussing who was surplus to requirements and could be left behind to make room for the very valuable chair. However, luckily the driver managed to squeeze it in pivoting it on the back seat and over the cases so that it went over Edward's head. When I say it went over Edward's head it did indeed fit, but only if Edward folded himself in two at the waist for the remaining eleven hours of the journey. When given the choice of being sold to the camel herding Disney operation or embracing his double jointedness and returning with us, Edward decided to return back to the hotel. This was, however, on the condition that he would inherit the chair in the event of our death, which may have been sooner than we thought as the car squeezed along the mountain roads with no guard rails and a sheer drop to one side. During our first meal back at the hotel, I was a little concerned that this had made the other boys decide it was worthwhile divvying up between them which bits of my stuff they will all get when we are dead, for fear of being the one left out. It was also clear when Dominic said that they could have my new chair as soon as I was gone, even if he was still around, that it may not have been his first choice of a purchase! It is times like this though that I knew I had married the right man as he struggled to bring back the chair he obviously hated, a huge bowl and a mirror. The chair didn't fit easily in any of the four cars we had to push it into or fit through any airport doors and there was some concern it may carry a high extra baggage charge, but he did not moan once.

When we arrived home I had a reply from my email to the CEO of Turkish Airlines. I had talked to the people at customer service to see if we could get our flights changed after Henry had to be rushed to the hospital, but they had told me that this was not possible and we would lose everything. Once again I had stood my ground, never one to be defeated, I went straight to the top and now discovered that he had arranged for us to have free flights to Istanbul well at least I thought they had because it was written in very unusual English. So it was Istanbul here we come!

I was so stressed checking everything twice to make sure there would be no mishaps and in a flash we were there. It was just as beautiful as I imagined as I looked out of my hotel to see the minarets of the blue mosque rising up behind the buildings on the opposite side of the old street to our hotel. It was not the amazing luxury resort we should have been in if we had made it the first time, but a more modest affair right in the centre of the old part of the city. Just when I thought things could not get any better I found out that one of my favourite cousins, Rachel, was there for the weekend too, up from Bodrum, buying wedding rings with her fiancé! We met them for dinner and they gave us the number of a friend who was a tour guide and would show us around and help us buy a rug without being ripped off like tourists. He took us to the Topeka Palace and the Blue Mosque, the Hagia Sophie and the Grand Bazaar. He took us to the market to purchase souvenirs and to a wonderful rug shop to make sure we had no money left to purchase the souvenirs! We visited Turkey at a somewhat turbulent time in the country's political life. While we were there, there were protests against the government of President Erdoğan, who many viewed almost as a dictator and was forcing the country into a less liberal nation. Although some protests were peaceful, others were not. During our visit, it seemed as though Turkish protestors had been asking James for advice on how to protest because they had a "read in" and blocked the streets by sitting and reading. What a wonderful way to protest I thought, blocking the streets soaking up knowledge. What could be more annoying to a dictator trying to force thoughts and ideas on to his people? Unfortunately, others took a more radical stance, and there were also riots.

Dominic needed to leave on a different flight than the rest of us, but when I packed his suitcase, it may have been a good idea for me to tell him that I had packed the gun that James had bought in the Grand Bizarre to add to his collection of medieval replica weapons. Maybe if I had when he was stopped to X ray his bags before entering the airport and security asked if he had a gun, he might not have answered, "No. Of course not." Then when they then opened his bags and found a gun, he would not have had to look so shocked and say, "Oh that gun! Yes, that's not a real gun!" If his behaviour had been less suspicious then maybe security would not have replied, "Well it looks real to us, so please step aside." If I had told Dominic about the gun then maybe he would not have been quite so terrified when armed security, in an airport of a country living under the threat of possible political rebellion, called in the head of security. Maybe terrifying scenes from the movie Midnight Express may not have flashed through his mind as he imagined himself thrown into a Turkish jail while he waited for the Security Chief to arrive. Luckily for him, the Head of Security recognised a fifteen dollar replica gun better than his underlings and Dominic was allowed to board the plane as long as his toy gun went in the hold. A few days later we returned home with nothing in our suitcases more dangerous than the Turkish delight that was guaranteed to put my diet in great jeopardy.

Morocco and Turkey were probably my two favourite places that we visited during our time in Germany. They were totally different from the European or American cities in every way. I loved Islamic cities that had been trading centres. The mixing of cultures leaves its mark on a place. Long after the traders have left, their spirits live on in the DNA of the city as their descendants inherit the quintessence of acceptance. We survived and came out stronger for it. Battling to be taken seriously and not overlooked as another immigrant grasping at services, not only makes you stronger, but also makes you understand the plight of those with greater struggles. I often wonder what happened to the Afghan man on my course as he struggled to learn German well enough to be able to replace his Auslander classes with a law classes and fight his way back to the status he had once had. I knew he would do it. His sort did. He was determined. He did not think he was owed anything yet The West owed him everything. He did not lament his previous life, but also he did not accept his new life. He moved on strengthened by his struggles and not discouraged by others' ignorance. He was an inspiration.

11 CREAKY BONES

Not all medical interactions were fearsome or tinged with guilt. Soon after arriving in Germany and after experimenting with a couple of unsuccessful options, a friend recommended that we try Dr. Kuna as our family doctor. It was a bit of a drive to get to him, but we were reassured it would be worth our while. We had called ahead and the receptionist was waiting for us as we turned up to register with him. We filled out the forms and handed them to her and were just about to leave when Dr. Kuna came out to call his next patient. A little old lady who could hardly stand, let alone walk struggled to her feet as her name was called. At this point Dr. Kuna heard us talking English to one another and realised who we must be so bounded over to welcome us to his new practice, leaving the little old lady stranded a few feet from her chair, quivering over her stick. He shook our hands vigorously, unaware that his next patient was fast approaching her best before date. He told us how excited he was to have us in the practice and that he was there whenever we needed him. The exuberance of our welcome was not confined to our first meeting. As soon as we arrived in the waiting room, packed with people who seemed in desperate need of the healing touch of Herr Dr.

Kuna, we would always be whisked into his room long before anyone else. It was only after a few visits we realised we were getting the star service. In Germany, there is socialised medicine, like the UK, so our private American health insurance was a welcome addition to Herr Dr. Kuna's coffers. Nevertheless, it did not sit easily with me to be rushed in before the elderly German patients who had worked and paid into the system all their lives. In the same way, I did not want to be treated as a second class citizen because of my immigration status, I definitely did not want anybody else to be. I just wanted equality and this superiority made me feel uncomfortable. Lack of equality fuels resentment of immigrants that could make my life difficult. They are taking our jobs, using our resources, taking our appointments at the doctors, so we will serve them last in the shops, embarrass them when they make small mistakes in grammar, or tell them to go back to where they came from when they express an opinion on our society.

Herr Dr. Kuna had beautiful crisp English with that Yoda type rhythm shared by all Germans, but his grasp of my language was not shared by any other medical professional we came in contact with. Before living in Germany I had assumed that all Germans spoke perfect English, and we would have no problems communicating. This was true in the city, but as you moved out to the surrounding villages, where we lived, it was less so. It was when we were dealing with medical issues that you needed the clearest communication. When the boys had their diving medicals, James had a slight cold so the doctor gave him a nasal spray and instructed him to "Put it in all his holes." Since the German for nostrils translates as nose holes, you can see how the doctor had made his best guess. Things were no better for Matilda when it came to finding her "appropriate holes". At her post op check, after shoulder surgery, the vet made his third attempt at taking her temperature and as he lifted her tail again he declared in his very German accent that, "This is very difficult for me to find the correct hole. She has a very hairy bottom!" Matilda just looked over her heavily bandaged shoulder with her, "Are you sure that's where you meant to stick it" face. Worse of all, he then suggested I cover the family thermometer with "the cream that has much grease" and have a go at home! Eventually, I came to learn that Germans seemed to solve all medical complaints by shoving something into a hole somewhere. On another occasion, the vet explained to me all in German that I needed to take a urine sample from the dog. I asked how? She obviously did not understand me so just repeated that I needed to take a urine sample from my dog, but this time louder and slower in that way that we all talk to foreigners who seem to not understand. I just repeated "Yes but how?" slowly and loudly to which she attempted to tell me I needed a urine sample from my dog this time in English. "I have understood you every time, but how?"

"Oh!" she said and presented me with a soup ladle duck taped to a broom handle. Alles Gut!

The doctor I visited for my foot was no exception to the communication difficulties. As I lay face down on the bed, with electric pulses zapping through my foot, I wondered if this was a real treatment to help with my heel pain or some crazy torture machine. Dr. Sauer, an eccentric, but kindly gentleman in his sixties cranked up the voltage as he told me how he loved the music of the late 60s and what a great time he had had in London in his youth. He spoke to me only in German, which meant I had to concentrate very hard on what he was saying, allowing me to zone out of the pain of the electric vibrations trying to break up the bone spur in my heal. Ever so often he would burst into song as a phrase or part of the conversation rekindled his memory. Then amongst all the German came sentences in English. "I remember a wonderful English woman I spent a few nights with, in 1968. Her name was Sue and she did things to me that no woman had ever done before or since. She was a wonderful woman!" His face lit up and he seemed energised by the memories of his sexual liaisons with the mysterious and talented Sue. His wife was his nurse and was working away in the corner of the room. She did not respond to his comment that no woman had stirred him since Sue, so I assume that she didn't speak English or maybe she had grown used to his ramblings. The conversation went back to German as he discussed the Beatles and the Rolling Stones, occasionally bursting into song. As he painfully injected cortisone into the sole of my foot, he asked if it hurt and when gasping for breath, I replied "Yeh Yeh Yeh", he again broke into song waving his left arm in the air and swinging his hips like Elvis whilst still injecting my foot with his right hand. I wished he would concentrate more on the syringe and less on his rendition of Georgie Fame and the Blue Fames, Yeh Yeh Yeh Yeh!

For some totally unknown reason, he was the doctor I chose to take James to when we were told his spine was not as straight as it could be and we needed to get it checked out. We were first directed into a room where James would be X rayed. The radiologist spoke no English, but informed us that the small pouch that she had handed me was to be placed over James's genitalia to protect it all from the radiation. I explained to James that he would need to wear this "willy protector" and that he would need to go in the cubicle to put it on. He looked horrified and confused and the more I looked at the tiny pouch the more I thought he really would not fit everything in there. I told the lady that I thought it was way too small and that my son was quite a big boy. I asked for a larger one only to be told that was the biggest one they had. James was mortified! German men must be very small I thought, but since James was now going redder and redder I decided to let him just try. It all seemed to fit and after the X-ray, the lady said "Kannst du bitter the Villy Protector in den Mull werfen" She smiled, very proud that she had learnt an

English word, but I did not have the heart to tell her that this was only a name I had made up for her small lead lined pouch. We then walked through to Dr. Sauer, who asked James to strip down to his underwear and stand with his back to him. As James bent forwards, to touch his toes as requested, Dr. Sauer again demonstrated he had a much better grasp of the English language than he made out. "Oh, Mein Gott!" He cried at the top of his lungs. "Kannst du Ski fahren? You must become a ski instructor! Many women would pay much money to ski down the mountain looking at those impressive buttocks!" There was not much one could say to that statement, so both James and I remained unusually silent, but smiled politely as though to thank him for the compliment. James gave me a "Get me out of here look," which implied that he was aware that his day really could get no worse. Soon his wish came true and he was to escape the crazy Herr Dr. Sauer for a prescribed a course of Krankengymnastics to strengthen the muscles around his spine. I, however, was not so lucky and was exposed to the pantomime and farce of Herr Doctor for many months to come.

Even when we returned to America medical appointments would quickly turn into a pantomime. At the boys' annual physicals the doctor suggested Edward had the HPV vaccine, but I said I would rather wait as at thirteen he was unlikely to be sexually active in the next year. Henry, who was only eight, piped up that he would like it because he was definitely planning to become more active in the following year! We decided that the sort of activity that Henry was intending was more likely to require a tetanus than an HPV vaccine, but that it was about time James had it. As the needle was thrust into James's arm he asked "Do I get a lego figure for my STD vaccine?" At that point, I realised that he was still more of a child than I had thought. That night, as STDs dominated the dinnertime conversation and the quandary of whether it's better to get a baby or syphIlis from having sex, I wondered if other families had similar conversations and if we would ever find a place where we just blended into the background. As they finished off their pasta and moved on to dessert the conclusion was drawn that it may be best to just not have sex at all.

My time in Germany taught me that, like education, healthcare was a compromise I would not make. I needed the best level of healthcare in order to feel safe, but I also needed to be treated as an equal to everyone else. Not better. Not worse. I did not want privilege and the uncomfortable feelings that it brought with it or the oppression of being the immigrant to be sent to the back of the queue as I was too much trouble to understand. Equality brings with it security and the feeling of unity and that was what I was searching for.

12 I JUST WANT TO BE UNDERSTOOD

America and England have been described as two lands divided by a common language. At times this commonality identified me as the right type of immigrant, who should be accepted and valued, but at others it separated me from those around me, identifying me as alien and threatening.

Nevermore was this evident than when we first arrived in the States and decided to install a new kitchen. The tap became the faucet, the worktop, the countertop, the hob the cooktop and skirting board the baseboard. Some words Americans found quaint or refined when I pronounced them differently, whereas manipulating the vowel sounds of other words caused total confusion. When I rang around for aluminium splash backs with the British pronunciation, containing all the syllables of al u min i um, I was told that they had never stocked such an item. Then I called again, on the advice of the kitchen installer, this time omitting sounds and over emphasising others to produce the American al oo min um, to find out that suddenly the same establishments now stocked exactly what I was looking for. It takes time to learn how and when you need to change and how you are going to be perceived based on your accent. The kids had similar problems. When Henry was attending an early intervention playgroup the lady running the group told me how well Henry talks. I pointed out that sometimes he screws up his face and talks like a deaf person sucking a gobstopper. She said that was perfectly normal with kids whose parents were foreign and he was just copying me!

Edward has always been a bundle of trouble. He was discharged from speech therapy just before starting preschool, since he could now say with confidence and clarity, "No way!" whenever he was asked to do anything. He spoke with an English accent, but used phrases like, "Give me five man!" which was both cute and annoying. On one occasion I was sat outside the tiny room in the local elementary school in which the speech therapist was working with him. I would listen in to fill the time, silently taking in what was happening, and sometimes giggling at the confusion the differences in language created.
"Edward where do you wash your hands?" I heard her ask.
"In the toilet." he replied. A perfectly good answer for an English boy, but she did not know that.
"Edward don't be so silly. You don't wash your hands in the toilet!"
"Yes I do!"
"No you don't. Where do you wash your hands?"
"In the toilet!"
"No, you don't!"
"Oh yes, I do!"
Before the whole thing turned into a complete pantomime I knocked gently on the door and explained to the, now slightly irate, speech therapist that he did actually wash his hands in the toilet it was just that she called the toilet the restroom.

In Germany, things were easier. I assumed language would always be a problem so I practised scenarios in my head ahead of time. If I said this they may say this or this then I will say this. This seemed to work most of the time.

Sometimes words just got so muddled up in my mind that phrases from one scenario filtered into others. I became so used to asking for Dominic's shirts to be washed and ironed that when I rang the dog groomer to get Matilda washed and dried, I asked for her to be washed and ironed! I was told that they could not do this any day so I hung up, but later that day, it suddenly dawned on me what I had said and I rang back to discover that they had lots of appointments!

In America and England, it was different. They assumed we spoke their language and it could leave you feeling imprisoned by a tongue that can bring social ruin in a single stroke. Standing in the line to pay for my groceries in Stop and Shop, trolly piled high with chlorinated meat and hormone pumped milk, James, then only four, decided to be helpful and bring social isolation all in one question, as he loudly shouted across the supermarket.
"Mummy don't forget daddy has run out of rubbers again."
Around me gasps as eyes bore into me from all directions and it was only my quick thinking reply of, "Remember dear. We call rubbers erasers in America," that prevented the arrival of social services to remove the poor innocent child from the depravity in which it was assumed he was raised.

It was the same in England, only worse, because I also had the accent that showed them I belonged, that I should know the right words. As a child when my Auntie Edith, the black sheep of the family, returned from America for a family wedding and asked for the water cooler in Marks and Spencer's, she was condemned by some of the family for making a spectacle of herself.
"She knows we don't have water coolers here. She lived here long enough. She is so attention seeking!"
But now I understood. Things change in your own country. When she left we were still using the imperial

system, but she had adapted to the new metric system, paying for 100 grams of sweets with the new coins she had brought for her visit, so why would we not also have changed to install water coolers in department stores. If you weren't there you can't predict the changes made in your absence, but if you have never been absent, never left the town in which your DNA was entrenched, you don't appreciate this. Even asking for an awake tea in an English Starbucks was a signal that I was not one of them. I had no way of knowing that this big corporation was more in touch with cultural norms than I was and had chosen to give different names to the same tea in different countries. I realised I would always be alien in both my old and new homes. I would never fit in anywhere again.

Every time my children used an American word for something on our trips home it would be pointed out immediately even before they had finished their sentences. What they said was of no importance, only how they said it. Using the word trash instead of rubbish was seen as a rejection of their own culture to be condemned. "They are English they should use English words." We were told by the same people who told us "all these immigrants coming over here should learn to speak English or go back to Poland or Romania or wherever else they have come from." We needed to speak their English even though we were visiting from a place that spoke another English, and needed to speak their English wherever we were in the world or else we had rejected our roots. However, those from other places must reject their roots and embrace their new British culture.

These contradictions are not peculiar to one culture or another. All cultures I have seen use implied rules to suit their own agenda. American's avoid confrontation at all costs. They are raised on the whole to question very little and to accept certain rules and conventions as set in stone. We were told that this allows a nation of immigrants to bind as one for the common good. It has purpose, a positive purpose. However, coming from a country with a constitution that is unwritten and fluid, where buses and queues in the supermarket are filled with total strangers debating and questioning everything in order to evolve and improve, it was very difficult to move to a land so devoid of argument and counterargument. In England at the height of the Brexit debate, just buying a large volume of cold remedies was enough for the checkout guy to launch headlong into a rant about how it was ridiculous to suggest that Britain would not have enough medications to supply its own people and there would be shortages after we left the European Union. He sited the Astra Zenica plant in his hometown of Loughborough as being more than capable of fulfilling all our medical needs, but he obviously hadn't returned home in a while since he seemed unaware that the plant had closed nine years earlier when production had moved to Sweden.

In America, it was taboo to question. Our district had some of the best schools apparently, but if I asked why they were the best I was told they came high up in the league tables, but any debate as to what the league tables made this decision on was not welcomed. The first amendment may allow for "freedom of speech," but the right to speak freely comes with a gagging order that allows you to only use that right to say what is uncontroversially accepted. One day, people were talking about a recent lockdown at the towns high school when a threat had been made against the school. When I exercised my right to free speech to suggest the second amendment, may be robbing the children in our schools of the domestic Tranquility, general Welfare, and Blessings of Liberty also promised by the constitution, my comments were not a welcome addition to the debate. One of the men's faces turned purple, like a beetroot, as he informed me that I had no right to question what was in the constitution. This was a contradiction he seemed unaware to have just made. Surely, the first amendment of his beloved constitution gave me the right to question the second. Comments like "well guns have been an important part of our country since it was founded so you would not understand," made sure that I was aware of my position as an immigrant. I was American when I paid my taxes but an immigrant when I expected representation. It was no different when I returned to England. Any opinion on Brexit or other major topics, that still impacted me as a British citizen, were shot down with, "You don't live here anymore. It's nothing to do with you." My ability to work and live anywhere in Europe, for my children to study anywhere, for my mother to get the medication she needed, were all irrelevant apparently because I had rejected my own country for another. I belonged to neither one place nor the other. I was always alien, always other, but I was also creative.

When we visited England from Germany and filled up the car with petrol we would walk into the petrol station to pay with our German petrol card and inevitably told that it did not work. "You'll just have to use your credit card love," I was being informed by the spotty teenager sat behind the perspex screen in the kind of voice used for foreigners. European petrol has one main distinguishing feature from American gas other than the word used to describe it. It is at least three times the price! As American ex-pats, it was assumed that this would blow our minds and cause mental distress, so part of our relocation package had been that all our gas would be paid for whilst we were on the assignment. Cheaper than therapy, I think was their reasoning. Anyway, it was a lot of money to lose and I had no intention of putting it on my credit card again, but based on our first stop at the services I knew it was easier for them to just insist we put it on a card than try to figure it out. Well, it would be easier if I was English, but if I were German as my car registration plate suggested, that may tip the scales in my favour. "I have no card for to pay," I said in the abrupt syllables I had heard so many times from Germans wrestling with my native tongue. "Please try again," and I handed him back the card. Again it did not work and again he said now even more slowly and loudly, "No you need a credit card"

"I have creditkaten" I said handing him back the card and smiling hopefully. The line behind me was growing and there was a lot of huffing of motorists eager to get on their way. He picked up the phone next to him in desperation. "I've got some German woman here and she hardly speaks any English. Says she hasn't got a credit card, but she's got a petrol card thing, but it won't go through."

He listened to the reply then said, "I think its Shell mate. Yep there's a number on t' back."

"Ok I'll try, but it won't work"

"Oh it did. Thanks mate see ya later."

Soon the receipt was growing out of the back of the machine and the petrol was paid for by the card that would not work. Every time I needed to do anything that I knew may not be immediately obvious to the cashier, be it my lack of chip and pin or a German gas card I would utilise the fake German accent and all would be well. Sometimes being alien is not enough. You need to be the right type of alien!

Dominic's fake German accent was little use to him when we were actually in Germany. He had made some vague attempt to learn the language, but did not stick at it beyond a few sessions with the language tape. I feared someday he may be arrested as he made mistakes, but the unforgiving Germans somehow seemed to forgive. One day he came after work to meet me and the children at the pool. He had only come to pick us up so did not have his swimming trunks, but had arrived early and wanted to see the boys enjoying themselves splashing around with their friends and maybe get a beer and sit with me on the grass. You only needed to pay to swim, so when he arrived at the kiosk to pay he told the guy on the gate that he didn't need to pay.

"I do not want to swim," he told him "so I do not need to pay. I am just here to look at boys!"

Worryingly the guy just nodded said an "Alles Gut" and buzzed him in.

Eventually, Dominic figured out German word order by realising that Germans use the same word order as Yoda. "Dominic can good German speak!" but his lack of vocabulary continued to create problems. He could ask for a beer or a sausage and anything else he believed was important, but his lack of a broader grasp of the language could have ended our marriage if I had been a less understanding kind of wife. His inability to even try to navigate the vernacular led me to believe that he may want to finish our relationship and for me to find a new husband when my Valentines day card, (all in German) covered in red hearts translated to read, "All my dreams have come true now you are both a couple. Wishing you lots of happiness in your new marriage!"

At first, I tried to help him all I could, but he seemed disinterested believing he had bigger fish to fry. I got to a point where I just let him struggle in the hope that he would see the need, but I am sure I could have been more supportive of his attempts to master the language as I laughed so hard at his attempts at telephone banking, that Edward ran in carrying the sick bucket in case I threw up. By the time we left, speaking German became much more automatic to Dominic, but this automaticity brought its own problems.

Just before we returned to the States, at the end of our three years in Germany, we made a quick trip to the invisible church in Belgium. Friends had said it was beautiful and a real "must-see". We arrived in the little village that the internet said contained the church, but there was no sign of it anywhere. Although it was called the invisible church, it was not, like the emperor's new clothes, totally invisible! The pictures showed it high on a grassy hill surrounded by fields. It was really an art installation known as "Reading Between the Lines" and was constructed of steel slats so that as you walked up the hill the steel was angled in such a way that the walls appeared to be solid. As you reached the top of the hill and stood on a level with the church you could see through the slats, so that the church seemed to fade into the Flemish countryside that surrounded it with maybe just a flash of sunlight reflecting off one of the steel surfaces to remind you that it was still there. As we wandered around the village though none of this was evident and there was no sign of the church or any clue as to which of the fields that surrounded the village contained it. Dominic decided to ask a lady tending her garden for directions in what he thought was French, but German had become so automatic to him he was actually talking German to her. Therefore, of course, the lady replied in German. Dominic then turned to me and loudly enquired in English why she kept talking in German? She then told him in English she could answer him in French, English or German, but could he please just decide which language he was speaking!

I like Dominic had totally lost my ability to speak French and, although when I attempted to speak all the nouns were correct, all the conjunctions, verbs and small words in the sentence became German, meaning that neither the French nor the Germans had a clue what I was saying. It was like I only had one box in my brain for foreign languages and they all just became muddled up if I attempted anything other than German. Language became neither natural and automatic nor challenging and well, foreign. I found myself thinking in German and answering in German even when we were back in America without really realising it. The same happened to Henry who when doing math would talk to his American teacher in German.

His special ed teacher had German parents and was a wonderful woman who totally understood what it was like to be raised in a cross-cultural environment and so she would just reply back to him in German whenever they did math.

The boys had German at school, but mastered it at different levels. James was far from fluent and when he did a role play as part of his lesson his German teacher complimented him on how well he played the idiot, even though that was not his intention! Henry was the most proficient and Edward at times lacked enthusiasm, which was not helped by the British voting to leave the European Union. Just as Britain could start to feel superior over America's stupidity in electing Donald Trump, they hit an all time level of dimwittedness by voting for Brexit. Edward told me there was no point in continuing his German lessons because we had left the EU, but after hearing him discuss Brexit with his German tutor, I decided it may be best for him to continue in the hope that he would speak German, not Denglish! "Wenn ich habe mine Großemutter gefragt welche way hast du gevoted sie hat gesagt mind dein bloody business!" When he asked why people voted to leave, I told him that they had voted with their hearts and not their heads, which may not be a good way to make an important choice.
"Yes apart from when you get married" he replied.
I disagreed "When dad asked me to marry him I asked for a week to think about it because I wanted to make the decision with my head. I thought that he was a hard worker and very smart and would look after us all because he always brought me breakfast in bed and he can make a good shepherds pie and puts us first."
"So you didn't choose him with your heart or your head then. You chose him with your stomach like most things didn't you?"
I really could not argue with his assessment of the situation.

We tried to help the boys along by joining German scouts and rugby and German summer camps, but I think all this, at times, just stressed them out. By the time they left though they knew that erect nipples were Igelnasen or, in direct translation, hedgehog noses, and amazing breasts were Porschetitten. They knew that when they were saying "pick your nose" in German it was not a boner in the nose which let's face it was probably physically impossible, but was in fact "bohrte in die Nase" or to bore into your nose. Edward knew that "elastic gymnastics" was not German for physiotherapy, but it was Krankengymnastics and only after living in a country and spending two hours being apparently rubbed all over by a cabbage, do I realise how similar the German words for cabbage and herbs are and that maybe it wasn't cabbage that I had been smeared in!

Every day became a new learning experience and at times it could be overwhelming, but at others it was exhilarating. Only after having your phone shout out "testicles" in a doctors waiting room do you learn that putting words on posters in a medical setting into google translate and pressing the speak button, to see if it was pronounced with a soft or hard "O", was probably not the best way to blend in as a local. Only by learning the national anthem, as I did for every country I had lived in, do you realise that unlike Wales and America some countries have two versions and it is best not to learn the Nazi one and start singing it loudly at school events! As Edward says making mistakes may be embarrassing or scary at the time, but it gives you a lot of good stories.

Our time in Germany definitely gave us plenty of tales to tell, but I also feel it helped us all to feel comfortable out of our comfort zone. Every day brought unexpected adventures. We had to just figure out how to get by, how to survive, so when we got back to America everything seemed easier, because at least we could explain our problem even if they saw it from a different cultural perspective. We learnt to stand up to bullies because the German way is often to just bully people into doing what you want. We found inventive ways to deal with bad German drivers who drove an inch from our bumper flashing their lights. The kids would all turn around and stare at them out of the back window endlessly, without smiling until they were so freaked out they moved back so they couldn't see the scary kids anymore!

I realised that being understood is about far more than others understanding the words you use. It is about them understanding the sentiment behind those words and these sentiments can be lost in the cultural confusion that exists if people are unfamiliar with where the other is coming from. The German removal truck driver who told me my husband was a "catastrophe" did not mean to upset me or belittle my choice of life partner. He just wanted to express his frustration at our inability to communicate and find a solution to his truck not fitting our street. Bluntness was culturally a norm for him. The Americans who describe their president as the leader of the free world don't mean to imply that all other countries are not free or are in some way lesser to their own. This phrase for them is a cultural norm. They are not actually meaning to express the implied sentiment, but it is my cultural norms that are causing me to falsely interpret that sentiment. Living in other places allows you to see that communication is culturally driven. When you understand this you begin to appreciate peoples' differences and embrace them, rather than feeling threatened by them. When we got back to America and became the right type of immigrant again, I realised that my time in Germany made me identify more as an immigrant than a white person. Although I would not experience discrimination to the extent that most black and Latino people do in America, I did understand what it was like to be frightened that your immigration status may cause you to not have access to the healthcare you need. I did know what it was like for my children to be disadvantaged educationally because of choices I had made, and the guilt that that brings. I did know how it felt to be judged for the place I was born, not the person I was and I hoped that now I was even more empathetic for those with even greater struggles than my own.

13 SOBERING UP SANTA

Father Christmas is not from Texas! He drinks whisky not milk and loves pies packed full of dried fruit, not an overly sweet cookie oozing with chocolate chips. He leaves gifts on Christmas Eve stuffed into a sack lying expectantly by the fire and never comes early to pack sweaty shoes full of chocolate. Or so I thought as I sat in the drizzle that permeated your soul in a Lancashire village, gazing at cards on a windowsill depicting a perfect snowy wonderland that would be washed away if it sat on the other side of the glass. Experiencing other cultures does not just bring struggles it opens your eyes to new joys, and nothing shows this more than the wonders of Christmas in the three countries we inhabited.

Our own traditions were enriched by those of each country we lived in and meant that Christmas seemed to go on forever. As Thanksgiving was added to our list of celebrations, Christmas began a little earlier to ensure no break in the festivities. The remaining Thanksgiving turkey loaded into sandwiches heralded the arrival of Stanley the Elf who moved every morning following his trip back to the North Pole to report on if the boys had been good or bad. This was also the day that the book advent calendar began. Each night the boys took it in turn to open a package that contained a bedtime story, some chocolate, a Christmas tree decoration and a note which had written upon it, either a joke a forfeit or an explanation of a fun activity planned for the following day. The books were eagerly anticipated and the boys became familiar with the stories over the years. Indeed, many of them they had written themselves, be it James's "If you Give an Elf a Nerf Gun" Edward's "Adventures of Stanley the Elf" or Henry's "Lego Santa and the Portal of Doom". I had even written a story myself about Stanley the Elf's struggles with dyslexia when all the other elves became sick. The boys' grandparents had recorded Hallmark Christmas books. Dominic's parents had loving read the story of the nativity and it was lovely to hear his mum's best school teacher voice telling of Mary and Joseph and the baby Jesus. My mum really did not see the point in the whole thing, having no sense of nostalgia whatsoever, but this only added to the fun. The boys would wait eagerly to hear the story of Frosty the Snowman read by a woman who made it quite clear, by the tone of her voice, that she herself was extremely frosty and thought the whole thing was totally ridiculous. "Thump, thump, thumpety, thump thump," she read obviously annoyed. "Thump, thump", she read before pausing for a frustrated sigh and continuing in an increasingly angry voice. "Thumperty, thump, thump". The boys would giggle and repeat their grandma's words trying to imitate the Grinch-like qualities of her voice.

When December the first arrived the traditional advent calendars would begin. My mum had sent red, green and white material ones from England, onto which I had embroidered the boys' names. Each calendar had pockets for each of the 24 days leading up to Christmas because we could not buy the chocolate ones in America, like you got in England, so we needed to fill these ourselves. We would all write six notes to each of the other family members so one could be placed in each of the pockets with a chocolate. Each note would contain something that the writer would do for the recipient over the following year, such as I will clean your room or I will bring you breakfast in bed. Notes written by dyslexics, however, were not always the easiest thing to understand. James offered to "Clean my ear". Further investigation revealed that the E should have been a C and it was my car that would receive his attention! Henry took a few years to fully understand the philanthropic nature of the cards. Until he did, we received pledges to play Lego for one million hours with us or to be allowed to stay up until midnight with him. Not sure how this would have benefitted me, but he assured us that he believed that was just what we would want.

It was also about this time that the boys would write their letters to tell Father Christmas just what they would want for Christmas. Some requests like Lego or games were easy for the elves to source, but others like James's request for a new belly button, Edward's desire for a basket of unusual fruit or Henry's for a talking hamster took a little more work or imagination. Edward's letter to Santa that began with, "I can explain!" and ended with "so I hope that we can overlook me buying three giant chocolate Santas with my lunch money," needed a little more explaining so we took them to the Mall. where each year they would meet Santa and make sure that he had fully understood their requests and confessions.

Excitedly and expectantly, we would stand in the line behind all the other children dressed in their best dresses, or a shirt with a bow tie, all colour coordinated with their siblings waiting for a photo with the man himself. As my boys sat on his knee, he recalled that they had visited him the previous year in a broad Texan accent. It never seemed quite right to me that Santa talked like this. Growing up he had always definitely been Lancastrian. The Mall Santa did

111

have a beard that had the texture of real whiskers and was definitely grown by the man himself. This was unlike the Lancastrian Santa of my childhood, who had a beard with the texture of nylon, firmly held in place with elastic loops. It stretched over his ears and regularly fell out of place to reveal the bare chin of a middle aged man from the Rotary Club. It always amazed me how Texan Santa remembered my boys, as he must see hundreds of children, each one only remaining on his big velvet green chair for a matter of minutes before the camera clicked and the next family were ushered in, but he definitely did remember them! The first time they met him they told him that they would not forget to leave him his whisky, which provoked a puzzled look for a man who was used to the promise of milk and cookies. Edward added that he knew he had milk and cookies when he came to American houses, but that was just because he was so drunk from his time five hours earlier in England that he needed a bit of dairy to sober him up. Santa was reassured by a nod from me and Dominic and a reminder to the boys from us that they must also remember the mince pie and carrots for Rudolf and his friends. I think Texan Santa was impressed by the English choice of beverage because he would mention it every year from then onwards. He always reminded them to be good boys and not to forget the whisky, even though they did not remind him that there would be no milk at the Gostick house. Edward used Santa's drinking as an alibi for his own Christmas crimes informing us that "Father Christmas doesn't flush when he has a wee because he'd wake everyone else up."

"Father Christmas doesn't have a wee."

"He does! He drinks all that whisky so he must have a wee."

"Yes but you do need to flush Edward!"

Soon after Thanksgiving, the tree needed to be purchased and this was always a bone of contention between Dominic and I. Neither of us had grown up with a real tree. We had a plastic tree whose branches needed to be inserted into the two-piece brown plastic trunk that sat in a three-pronged stand. Each year, from the year I was born, when my grandparents had brought the tree for me, a plastic twig would become detached and we would search for the stub it should be reattached to. My dad would disappear into the shed to fix the lights and return moments later with a twinkling sting to bring the plastic tree to life. Dominic's dad also had broken lights to repair every year, but he was not so technically proficient with electrical items as my dad so Dominic recalls yearly stress and argument as their golden tinsel tree was erected and illuminated.

When it was time for us to get our own tree, Dominic loved to go to Trombetta's ice-cream and garden centre where you would select a pre-cut tree and then sit and eat ice cream whilst the tree was strapped securely to the top of the car by Mr. Trombetta. As soon as you had lapped up the scraps of black raspberry, chocolate or coffee from the bottom of the enormous paper tub with the festive red plastic spoon, and maybe bought a poinsettia or two, it was all ready for you to drive off hassle free.

I, on the other hand, preferred the long drive to a tree farm in Grafton where you were given a large tarp and a saw and pointed in the direction of the field full of trees in the distance. You would then march off through the snow to choose a tree. After much discussion, the tree was selected. Dominic would lie on the frosty, wet ground to saw away at the trunk, snow falling in clumps on his bareback from the long branches of the fattest tree in the field until it fell. He would lift it onto the tarp and drag it back to the car through the snow which would rise up over the top of his boots and melt against his skin before dripping down into his socks. He would then attempt to lift the wet spiky branches onto the top of the car, before strapping it on with string, whilst the boys and I went into a warm hut for hot cider and cookies and to pay. To me, this was a much more romantic way to begin the celebrations, but for some reason, it was less appealing to Dominic, so we would alternate between the tree farm and Trombetta's, until we went to Germany and everything changed.

The Germans lit their trees with real candles. Therefore, they would not buy trees until the few days before Christmas to make sure the needles remained fresh and giant pines did not ignite in their living rooms into a festive fireball. We would travel to England, though a few days before Christmas, so needed a tree much earlier in the season than they were available in the shops. Friends who had lived in Germany for several years before us however, assured us that they knew of a tree farm a little way south of Frankfurt where you could cut down your own tree from the start of December. In our first year in Germany, we all set off in a huge ex-pat convoy down the motorway on the first weekend of December. The friends had told us it was a bit of a drive, but we had not expected two hours at lightning German autobahn speeds. It felt like we were almost in Austria when we saw the sign for the farm. Everyone bundled out of their cars and headed for the little hut where a man pointed us towards what seemed more like a cliff face than a field of trees. Clinging on the side of the rocky slope were the saddest collection of trees you had ever seen. Each one of them had received no light from behind, where the land rose sharply blocking out the sun. The only light came from across the valley and meant that the trees had one beautiful bushy side and one totally bald side. We all scrambled up the bank clinging on to the grass to prevent ourselves from slipping back down towards the car park. We found the least twig-like tree that we could, that had a small area with some semblance of greenery and life clinging to its branches and Dominic attempted to saw through the trunk. Since the ground rose up sharply behind the trunk this was not an easy task as the saw banged against the rocky slope. This was a piece of cake in comparison to trying to get the tree safely down the vertical path towards the hut to pay.

Eventually, Dominic managed to wrestle the tree down spending as much of the decent on his bum as his feet. He strapped it to the car and I went to pay. I did not dare to tell him the cost. As the only tree farm, it seemed in the whole of Germany, supplying crazy foreigners who wanted trees weeks before the big day, the owners were more than aware that they were a monopoly that could charge a premium. Suddenly, even the Grafton tree farm seemed appealing to Dominic and the journey back along the autobahn only added to this appeal. If the journey there had taken two hours travelling at 90 miles an hour the journey back with a half-dead skeleton of a tree strapped to the roof was to take much much longer. Even I failed to see the romance of the experience, as we positioned the tree in the corner of the living room so that there were two walls to hide its lack of foliage. The following year we bought a plastic tree that we continued to use back in America. I always wanted a tree with coordinated decorations and beads, but the rest of the family preferred tinsel and a hotchpotch of decorations collected from our travels and made in preschool classrooms. Thus, the plastic tree became the home to tinsel, baubles with pictures of European cities and two lollypop sticks framing photos of three year olds in Santa hats and reindeers made of tiny handprints.

When we returned from Germany, Dominic's days of watching over the top of his ice-cream cone as a Trombetta tree was strapped to the top of his car, were well and truly over. Edward had started work at a tree farm in Southborough. The elderly couple, who owned it, had been looking for a new boy scout to help them out there as the old one had gone off to college. Nate Hall an old friend of James's from Kindergarten and boy scout, had mentioned it to Edward and he was now an apprentice tree farmer. This meant that there was an expectation that we would buy our tree from the farm and so we dutifully went off to tag a prize specimen. The lady who owned the farm was a no messing kind of New Englander who treated Edward really well, but had high expectations

One year our friend asked us to take them to the farm, so that Edward could help them to buy their tree. They came over and had lunch and then we prepared to go to the farm. They both had normal shoes so we managed to find them some wellingtons and they fought to pull them on their feet. As we arrived at the farm we were directed on to a field used for parking that butted up to the big red barn where Deidre sold Christmas ornaments and quilts. Maurice and Deidre had set up the Christmas tree farm for their retirement and now the couple who were probably in their mid seventies used young workers, that they normally recruited from the scouts, to do the heavy work and help them in the busy Christmas season. Deidre had long white hair normally tied up in a bun or in a ponytail that fell down her back and was a force to be reckoned with. Maurice was an easy-going chap who smiled a lot and did as he was told. He had a few health problems and was regularly chastised for overdoing it by his life long love and the boss. Maurice directed us through the newly fallen snow to the front of the barn and went in. It was beautiful with two rooms off to the left selling fall decorations and gifts. A large area ahead of us had trees covered in handmade ornaments from all around New England. To your right as you came in was the cash register and jars of farm-produced honey some jars flavoured with herbs also grown on the farm. Beautiful wreaths covered the walls decorated in baubles which Edward and the other workers twisted together on quiet days when the weather was bad. In baskets sat pouches of catnip lovingly stuffed by the three boy scouts the farm employed. As we chatted to Deidre a Mercedes Jeep pulled up outside the barn. As it drew to a stop its occupants were welcomed in by Deidre as Maurice walked over to direct them to the right area. Two dark-haired women in their twenties got out and headed to the barn, tottering on the high heels of their designer boots, whilst the two men who accompanied them took a drone out of the back of the Jeep, watched eagerly by a white handbag dog with a bow in its hair.

The two glamorous young women entered the barn and took out a video camera. One of the women walked around the barn looking at all the things on sale, giggling, smiling and talking in excitable Spanish, as her friend filmed it all.

"What are they doing?" Deidre asked, obviously annoyed that they had not asked to film her barn. Maurice came in to inform her that the two men were putting together a drone with a camera to film the fields of trees and this only added to her annoyance.

The new customers definitely did not fit the farm's normal demographic of local families with excited children or older couples whose excited children had now grown into nonchalant teenagers or young adults recently flown the nest. This group were glamorous, twenty somethings with money to burn and large black fur hats but unsuitable footwear. Their unusual behaviour upset Deidre and she was obviously concerned with their intentions, as we all were. My friend and I took in on ourselves to take on the role of interrogator and asked the women where they were from. She told us that she had a Youtube channel called, "El Mundo De Camila" and they were filming for their next episode. Each episode was viewed by about 200,000 viewers she told us. As they tottered out and headed off into the fields with Edward, the two men ran behind them, stripped of their drone during a negotiation with Maurice, who had agreed to a small drone session before they headed to the trees.

"Ridiculous boots for a farm!" was Deidre's parting comment and festive farewell.

When the Youtube episode entitled, "Christmas Has Come To The Funny Family Of The Puchis" aired, Edward made sure that everyone now knew he was an internet sensation, even though he was only there for a few minutes. He took his role as the friendly face of the farm very seriously and would put his occupation on forms as lumberjack or farmer. A few months of working as an elf on a Christmas tree farm and he thought he was Old MacDonald!

The start of December really was a busy time because, not only did advent calendars need to be opened, Father Christmas provided with wish lists and a tree needed to be purchased but after living in Germany shoes needed to be left out for St. Nicholas. Each year as I filled the sweaty shoes, ever-increasing in size, needing more and more chocolate to fill them, I would think of our first Nikolaus. Other seasoned parents at the school told us how the children would place their shoes outside, by the door, to be filled by Nikolaus on the eve of his saints day. This first year I had little notice that large amounts of chocolate would be required and even less notice that I would need to purchase it on Nikolaus's behalf, so I cobbled together a few bits and pieces I had put on one side for stockings. Each pair of shoes was dutifully placed outside the door as three excited boys disappeared up the stairs to dream of the magical figure, loaded down by a sack of their favourite treats. In reality, only one English chocolate bar was placed in each of the six shoes as a weary mother climbed the stairs to dream of disappointed children. The next morning, however, each shoe was overflowing with German chocolate and gifts cascading out on to the concrete below as three boys stood wide-eyed before gathering up Nikolaus's bounty. That morning the real magic of the season was there for all to see, the naivety of a child and the kindness of neighbours keen to welcome newcomers. Soon leaving out our shoes for Nikolaus became part of our multicultural Yuletide, that bore little relation to Dominic and my childhood festivities.

My Christmas as a child was very low key being an only child, but burst into chaotic excitement on Boxing Day. This was when all of my aunts, uncles and cousins squashed into a tiny house to be force fed meat and potato pie, mushy peas, trifle and coconut slices, whilst being forced to join in the screeching out of carols in a variety of keys. My dad's parents had been married on Boxing Day and, since my Nanna always worked at the hospital on Christmas Day, Boxing Day became the day for Croasdale celebrations. After my Nanna died, my Dad and his brother and sisters took it in turn to host the Boxing Day party. The menu was always the same. Whoever held the party made a huge meat and potato pie. Marie always brought mushy peas, Sandra the trifle, our family coconut slices and Auntie Helen, wimberry pie and damson gin.

At first, we all got presents off each family, but as the numbers grew it was decided that each person would be given one other to buy for. The presents would not be distributed until everyone had sat and sung carols together from crinkled carol sheets that reappeared every year. My dad, as the eldest, would lead the carols and make the final decision of when enough singing had been completed to earn our gifts. He would then pick presents one by one from under the tree and yell out the name of the recipient who would step over cousins, nieces and newly arrived spouses to claim their prize. My family was possibly the worst singers in the world! Each of my aunts sang out of tune, but in totally different keys. They would all criticise the others, unaware that their own talents were equally lacking. However, this was all part of the day, part of the tradition. Dominic's family also believed themselves to be excellent singers so, when Dominic attended his first Boxing Day party and attempted to sing like he was in a church choir, he was quickly brought into line with cries of, "Oh 'eck who does he think he is? Michael Bouble?"

When we were living in America and Germany I would still Skype to join in the singing to feel part of it all. It was one of the things I think I missed out on being away from home and it filled me with sadness that my children missed out on cousins and family.

One year my attempt to compensate for this loss brought friends to our home in Germany, some carrying musical instruments to experience the mysteries of Boxing Day. Toake placed her sushi on the buffet table, Laurie added a multilayer Mexican dip and the Chadwick's a South African dish, as a huge pot of meat and potatoes bubbled on the stove awaiting its pastry top and side of mushy peas. As each person arrived and asked the same question, nervous of what was to come, we explained that Boxing Day had nothing to do with glove wearing sportsmen, but was actually the day the wealthy gave their servants a box of treats to take home for the day to celebrate Christmas the day after they had to wait on their employers. Once the children had gathered around Toake and been taught how to assemble their own sushi and the pot of meat and potato pie has been stripped of its contents and left in the sink to soak, it was time to Skype. Crisp new carol sheets were printed out from the scanned copy sent from this year's British host and handed to waiting hands in Dreieich. As my cousin appeared on the screen I could not hold in my excitement anymore as the iPad was handed round the crowded Blackburn living room for each family to wish me a Happy Christmas. At that moment, I was in Blackburn too despite being a thousand miles away. I chatted with cousins unaware of the faces around me. As I looked up to see if everyone was ready to sing, I was greeted by silent, concerned faces as Barry's deep booming voice pierced the silence.
"What's happened to Kate? It is like she has had a stroke!" he laughed.

"Yeh! Why is your mum talking with a funny voice?" Barry's son asked Edward. So sure was I that I was back home that I dropped my guard and my own accent broke through shocking those accustomed to my toned-down neutral vowels necessary if I was to be understood in an alien land. It was the rest of the time I was putting on a funny voice. This is my real accent reserved for my own people. At this moment I was a melon in a crate of melons surrounded by an array of international fruits looking in from their tropical fruit celebration basket. My children and husband were part of the basket, but I was, at this moment, part of the crate and realised being part of the basket meant you needed to lose part of yourself. When you choose to join the basket you must leave a little of yourself behind in the crate.

Dominic felt our Christmas bore little resemblance to his Christmas as a child and was a kind of mix of our Christmases and my sister in law, Janet's. Dominic said he always left his pillowcase at the end of his bed and was allowed to explore its contents as soon as he woke up be it in his own house or the alternate year at his Gran and Grandpop's. My stocking was a sack placed by the fire and I was not allowed to open anything until we were all dressed and had eaten a substantial and lengthy breakfast. Now our stockings were by the fire and opened immediately on everyone being awake. This was in part that I had always hated the wait for breakfast, sitting at the table with the best silverware and a smart uncomfortable outfit, willing my mother to eat quicker. Therefore, as an adult when I had control, I would spend the whole day in my pyjamas and open the gifts as soon as we were awake. Dominic's breakfast on Christmas morning had always included a cold bacon joint accompanied by crusty white bread and tomato sauce. Tomato sauce was a substance that to the best of my knowledge has never crossed my mother's threshold, being a concoction purchased only by lower-class burger eaters!

Church was never a big part of my Christmas growing up, but Midnight mass was a big part of Dominic's and therefore became part of our celebrations. In America, they had a lovely service at about 4 pm which had the Sunday school performing a nativity, but this soon replaced midnight mass before returning to the more enjoyable early service as Edward informed us he did not like church here because everyone else got a drink and a snack and he just got hit on the head. We explained that it was a blessing for those too young to take communion, but he remained unconvinced. It did not help that we were always late. One year we arrived to find the church full and were directed into the choir stalls. It was bad enough being right at the front and feeling on full view, but to our horror, we realised that microphones were hanging above our head, piping our atrocious singing out into the congregation. This realisation resulted in a lot of elbows being dug into ribs signalling that this year it may be best to just mouth the words rather than inflicting the voice, the good Lord gave us, onto the whole community! Another year, Henry was invited to be an altar boy because they were really, really desperate. This was the child who referred to Jesus's parents as Mary and Jeff as he assembled the nativity scene on the table in the dining room before adding the three wise men, apparently carrying gold, Frankincense and milk. Maybe not the best choice for a major player in the Christmas religious experience! His once a year visit to church at Christmas was no real help either, but they explained what he needed to do. This at least meant that we arrived early enough to get a seat, but unfortunately gave plenty of time for Edward to list, in the loudest ever whisper, all the things that may go wrong from Henry cracking unsuitable jokes to him setting fire to the vicar with a stray candle. Luckily apart from dropping a bell at a fairly quiet time following communion, he managed not to ignite the vicar or crack any faux pars.

Even a trip to Lapland to see the "real" Father Christmas, showed my children's inability to be surprised. We had taken the older two there during our trip home for my mum's 70th birthday, a few months after moving to America. Even then Dominic had described it as Butlins in the snow! We were greeted at the airport by an elf with a Scouse accent who then transported us around the frozen wasteland by bus, husky sled, reindeer sleigh, and snowmobile shouting, "elf alert!" every time we passed one of his colleagues huddled around a fire dressed in a red and green elf costume. Our aim was not actually to be alert to the employees who had drawn the short straw making them sit in the sub-zero temperatures dressed in lycra being a woodland elf, but to spot Father Christmas. Obviously, it was going to be the final day that we got to meet him. Apparently, we had just missed him when we found his workshop in the woods filled with busy elves or when we sat in the snow covered tepee at the husky farm. Our disappointment came to an end though when he turned up with his reindeers on the last night for the party in the hotel. Dominic regularly pointed out that for the extortionate cost of the three days, in what he considered a frozen arctic theme park, we could have gone somewhere warm and nice. I loved it and it was all so magical to me. Racing across a frozen lake in a sled pulled by huskies under a pitch-black arctic sky with not a single glow of light pollution, snuggled under reindeer skin blankets with a two year old and four year old, to me could be nothing but magical.

I did not want Henry to miss out on this magic, so when we went back to England for our last Christmas before moving back to America, we decided to go, just Henry and I, to rekindle the magic. This time was even better because I got to drive the team of huskies through the pitch-black wood. I was driving the last team and since Henry and I were so light compared to the families of four huddled in the proceeding sleds we were the fastest team. I was terrified at times as we bolted into the darkness, ducking and swerving to miss the low hanging trees, but I was desperate to do it again. The next day, I was not sure Henry totally got the Lappish enchantment, however, after we were nestled under fur blankets in the sledge pulled by reindeer through a forest, the moonlight twinkling on the snowy branches, to a hut in the forest where we ate special buns and drank hot berry juice. As we pulled up outside to be greeted by people dressed in traditional dress Henry announced, "We'd have got here a lot quicker in a car!" He is, it must be said, his father's son! He did eventually come round and despite us swimming outside at -24 degrees centigrade, so our hair froze into icicles as we swam and we couldn't use the handrail because our hand stuck to it, Henry said it was his best holiday ever! The magic and charm even permeated into his dreams as I was woken by Henry screaming, "Get me more biscuits bakery elf" in his sleep. As we raced down the Autobahn with Dominic and the boys, after celebrating Christmas Day with Dominic's family, Boxing Day with mine and heading back to Frankfurt, I realised that during the previous two weeks we had slept in eight different beds and passed through six different countries and now all I wanted to do was sleep in my own bed in my own onesie.

Christmas trips home always seemed eventful and exhausting. They always included a stop in Brugge to wander the streets and visit the rickety old wattle and daub shop called Dumon's Chocolatiers. The tiny shop was easily spotted by the long line snaking out of the door on to the snowy streets. They waited to be admitted into the chocolate heaven, so small that it held only one family at a time in front of the counter piled high with creations straight out of Willy Wonka's factory. There were flavours that could not be dreamt of, whose delights could not be conceived of until they hit your tongue and the brilliance of strawberry and basil or orange and chilli became apparent. With a box of these perfect balls and cubes of chocolate clasped in one hand to share with family and a bag of chocolate covered orange rind for the journey, we would head off for a fondu lunch or an afternoon tea. The tea room was hidden away up the uneven wooden stairs in the shop that claimed to have the best hot chocolate in the world. Here clouds made of marshmallows accompanied a never ending cup of hot chocolate. One year we made the mistake of taking a box of the marshmallows home with us to allow family to experience their lightness, unaware that like clouds their existence was eliminated by time, so that all that remained was a smear of sugar at the bottom of the box.

Each year we would alter our route slightly to explore a different location. One year we travelled back through France to visit the grave of my Grandma's brother killed in World War one and the memorial to Dominic's great grandfather lost in the same conflict. This was the time we stayed in a beautiful chateau. It was in an area near the Somme and all through the countryside were tiny graveyards full of immaculate white crosses in neat rows. I had assumed there would just be a few large war cemeteries, but the reality were lots of tiny graveyards tended by locals and a commission set up to look after the graves. There were some large memorials and graveyards, but my great uncle, Robert Briggs, was to be found buried next to his Cumbrian friends and comrades with whom he was sitting in a mess tent when a shell killed them all. It seemed fitting that now they lay together not growing old, not being wearied by age, but being remembered by visitors from another time. Dominic's great grandfather on the other hand was killed and his body never found. As we drove up to the gate of the Pozier's Memorial, we could see a huge horseshoe shaped wall, engraved with hundreds and hundreds of names surrounding row upon row of more tiny, white, immaculate crosses each with the name of a son, a brother, a husband. We parked the car on the gravel area in front of the gate and, stopping to read the book on the way in, headed off to search for Wilfred's name amongst the fallen heroes on the wall. Just as we found the panel on which the book had said we would find his name, a French man in his 50s ran in towards us waving his arms and shouting. He was angry. His skin red and sweating, his brow furrowed and his eyes filled with hatred.

"Hello Is everything ok?" I said. As he continued to shout "Excusez moi?" I added hoping he would slow down so I could understand what he was saying. Suddenly he stopped dead in his tracks and enquired, "Anglais?"

"Oui" I replied.

Suddenly the urgency with which he had entered the cemetery seemed to have passed, his brow softened, his skin became paler and in his eyes, the hatred melted into confusion as the calmness returned.

Dominic, concerned for our safety had now reached my side as the man handed me an old bullet and said "Souvenir," as he turned and disappeared towards the gate with large determined strides. I placed the bullet in my pocket, found the name on the wall, took photos of the engraving to share with the family and headed back to the car. As we headed back to our big black BMW with the German number plate it suddenly dawned on us that the man would have assumed we were German. This may have explained the shouting in an area which even now, had a landscape showing the scars of the war that had taken place there a century ago, where the tiny cemeteries provided a constant reminder of the carnage the German's had placed on the local communities. The man had not been kindly bringing a souvenir for the descendants of a man who had given his life for his ancestors' freedom, but was instead returning a bullet, in his mind, to the descendants of a man who had tried to take that freedom. As we drove towards Calais, bullet in pocket, to the tunnel I reflected on how Dominic's Gran and my great grandmother had never had the chance to visit these memorials to people they had known and loved and how I am sure if they had it would have been a great consolation to know how well cared for their final resting places were. I also reflected on how the actions of our country or ancestors over which we have no control, which happened long before our arrival onto the world stage, shapes other's perceptions of who we are. Their guilt is inherited by their descendants as the judgment of those they persecuted is inherited by theirs.

On Boxing Day we saw my cousin and showed her the bullet. As a police officer, she was horrified to see her favourite cousin clutching live ammunition, totally unaware that it was a crime that carried a life sentence in Britain! She suggested we took it to the canal and threw it in, but I could not help but think that if it was found in the future by some archeologist they may incorrectly conclude that the Germans had had a gun battle as the locals defended the Leeds Liverpool canal, just outside Blackburn. We ended up taking the bullet back with us to Germany and then to America, but it was always a source of worry to me.

As the years passed the American style Christmas cards that we had now adopted with pictures of the perfect family in matching outfits were first replaced by cards with photos of two gangly spotty teenagers and a nine year old who is incapable of looking normal. Eventually they became the British style cards with a picture of a snowy scene with a well placed robin or a cartoon Santa. As my little ones paraded into the living room to leave out a mince pie, whisky and carrots for Father Christmas and his reindeer, all dressed in the elf pyjamas that they had discovered in the final package in their book advent calendar, they placed their sacks by the fireplace for Father Christmas to fill with everything their hearts desired. I began to wonder if the Christmas magic was beginning to fade as James informed me that he was now nineteen, over six foot tall, had a beard and was dressed as a "Sodding elf!" "When is this madness going to end Mother?" I pointed out that those who don't believe don't receive and the magic returned like a little sprinkle of fairy dust. The biggest elf got a new job loading all the presents into the younger elves Christmas stockings and the peace and tradition of the season was restored.

James did not seem to understand that Christmas for me was a whole host of memories that I wanted to recreate for them. So far away from the immediate and extended family that played leading roles in my Christmas memories, I worried that my boys would lose the culture that was so important to me. Mince Pies, Christmas puddings, Christmas cakes, all added to the heartburn from excessive dried fruit that makes up an English Christmas. Boxing Day and Christmas crackers, selection boxes and advent calendars were all not so familiar to Americans, although they were starting to permeate into the American psyche during the time we lived there. I wanted my children to have it all. I think it is as much the preparation for Christmas that gives me so much pleasure. The planning, the finding the perfect gift, the excitement of the kids on Christmas morning. In answer to James's question of when will this all end, I hope the answer is never!

14 NEW YEAR! NEW COUNTRY!

Time differences make parties last longer, allowing you to travel through time to celebrate the same time around the world all in one night. It's the trick Santa uses to deliver all those gifts you know. Even when traditions were the same in two countries we still managed to benefit from being an international family, as we celebrated in multiple time zones whilst existing at that moment in only one time and place. New Year's Eve seemed to last all day as we celebrated English New Year with English friends and five hours later American New Year with American friends. Boston kindly put on a parade that culminated in fireworks at 7 pm, allowing American families with young children to all be in bed long before midnight. In the beginning, we wandered the streets looking at the ice sculptures all around the city and then followed the parade from Copley Square to the Common, enjoying the bands and performers, people on stilts, baton twirlers and floats and marchers from local groups. At 7 pm, English New Year fireworks filled the sky over the Common, bangs echoing off the skyscrapers and bright colours reflected in their glass. We hugged our friends and rang our families and then set off home. We had a quick sit down and a cup of tea and then set off to a friend's house to bring in the New

Year with them, watching the ball drop in Time Square as we would have watched Big Ben chime twelve deep bongs at home. We then crossed arms much to the surprise of our American friends and sand a verse or two of Old Lang Syne, before the universal kisses and hugs. As the years progressed the parade and ice sculptures were replaced by a meal close to the Common on a table that stretched into the distance with British friends and their children. By now the Americans would cross hands as though this had been their tradition for generations and generations and then shake their arms vigorously up and down sharing the love around the circle.

Germany had its own traditions some we would attempt to adopt and others we were glad to leave behind. We invited friends over to celebrate the New Year and watched Dinner for One, a British black and white movie, unknown to British audiences, but loved by Germans every New Years' Eve as the Wizard of Oz in England or the Grinch in America. Freddie Frinton, who plays a butler, drunk from sharing a drink with his 90 year old employer with each course of a very long meal, ends the ten minute film with a wink in response to the old ladies comment of "Same procedure as last year," implying he won't just be tucking her into bed, but will climb in with her and help the year go out with a bang! Germans would often interrupt their German spiel with an English, "same procedure as last year", expecting us to understand the implied meaning, but this was a cultural reference for them, not us, even though it had come to them from the flickering black and white images of an English butler. This was not uncommon in America. Whenever my friend, Marcia, introduced herself she would be greeted with a smile and a quickly recounted "Oh Marcia Marcia" to which she would nod knowingly and share an unspoken memory. If I had greeted everyone named Betty with a Frank Spencer "OOOh! Betty," I would soon be referred to as the odd English woman, unless of course I too was

130

in England, where it would be echoed back in a quavering voice and joined by an, "I've had a bit of trouble. The cats done a woopsie on the carpet". Catchphrases unite people of the same generation and the same culture. My children were not united with their parents who were raised on another continent in another millennium and would respond to renditions of the Benny Hill song with a sigh and an observation of that "not being a thing."

In Germany at New Year, although it had never been a thing for us, we began melting the Bleigiessen, little pieces of lead shaped as hats or pigs or a whole host of random shapes. As it melted in the spoon you thought of the year to come before pouring the molten silver liquid into a glass of water, watching it solidify into a new shape. Great discussion then ensued as to what the new random shape was, a tree symbolising you would experience loyalty in love over the next year or a lantern to signal your upcoming moment of enlightenment. Maybe it was a bird telling you to move more, or an anchor telling you to make your safety a priority. The reality of the situation was that you should always see an anchor, as one's safety was soon to become a major priority as we all marched up the hill to the highest, darkest field in town.

I took the advice of the Bleigiessen in that I only climbed that hill once. Just that one year. What was there was one of the most terrifying things I had ever seen. Drunk German voices echoed out of the darkness, accompanied by the chink chink of beer bottles wishing good health to a friend, only a couple of feet away, whose shadow moved in the moonlight. You could not see the empty bottles being buried only an inch into the mud, the remaining six or seven inches protruding out of the dirt, a receptacle for death. It was only as the clock on the tower in the town wall struck midnight that the purpose of the bottles was revealed, illuminated by lighters igniting the wicks which hung down their sides. Bang! Bang!, as fireworks exploded from bottles all over the ground around us, swishing past us as they journeyed into the sky. Bang! Bang!, as the bottles fell and rockets flew not into the sky as intended, but along unforeseen trajectories, whizzing past jumping Germans and fleeing children. In America, the police would be called and warnings would be spelt out in the orange bulbs of motorway signs. In Britain a series of government sponsored advertisements would flash between favourite TV shows and judgmental tuts would be made of the perceived perpetrators over cups of tea, but in Germany, this was a yearly activity accompanied by raucous laughter and even more drinking. Fireworks were only sold between Christmas and New Year and it was illegal to set them off at any other time other than Sylvester, New Year's Eve. For some reason, the government saw the danger of giving drunken men explosives, but felt the need to allow an end of year purge of those who were not quick enough or sharp eyed enough to avoid explosives on sticks hurtling towards them through the cimmerian shadows. Fireworks had terrified me since I was little, when each year the second operation to remove a birthmark from my left cheek was put back as the paediatric plastic surgeons were too busy repairing the faces of children burnt by Bonfire Night fireworks. This left a new mark on me as I was left with penetrable fear of explosives in untrained hands. Needless to say, we melted lead and ate marzipan pigs holding clover and ladybirds and watched Dinner for One, laughing at its predictable farce, but the fireworks we left to the professionals on Boston Common.

15 SEX, DRUGS AND BILLY BOBS

We all have sex. With a few minor variations, we even all do it the same way. As Henry explained, "The man squirts Spain out of his willy into the lady's divina." So if we all do it the same way, why do our schools teach it so differently and why do we have such different attitudes?

As with most things, Germany and America seemed to lie on the two extremes with Britain taking the middle ground. I suspect, as with so many aspects of life, culture and tradition are the main shaping factors. Germans see that the sight of the nude body is completely normal, natural, a symbol of heath and vigour not sexuality. Hermann Goering, a leading figure in the Nazi party, described how the "healing power of sun and air" would make the strong nation and in East Germany naked bathing was used as a sign of dissidence, revoking the Culture Ministry's calls to "Protect the eyes of the nation". Comfort with their nakedness and an openness about sex is what makes them German. They are proud to show off their strength and become healthier by being closer to nature so the schools reflect this attitude and sex education began in Kindergarden becoming more and more comprehensive as students reached puberty

.

America was founded on puritan values which, although diluted through the years, still have a defining influence. Culture shapes what schools decide to teach us as they battle not to conflict with family values whilst educating their pupils to be able to safely become sexual beings. They need to consider the religious beliefs of families and differing views on the age that sex education should begin. My experience of American parents was that, on the whole, they assumed their children were abiding by their inherited, puritan philosophies, but in reality, they were not, just as their parents had not been guided by these philosophies in their youth. Double standards in a land of contradiction again raising its head. This assumption led the schools to again reflect the attitude of the community, providing the sparse sex education seen as sufficient and preferable, by families whose ideas were built on shaky foundations.

These family attitudes, however, needed to be balanced against the concern that students were taught critical topics too late, risking teenage pregnancy and sexually transmitted diseases but this did not always happen. As a result teenagers were often misguided about the facts and learnt from one another.

In America, sex education was given, in my opinion, far too late and was far from informative. For my boys, this was first breached in fifth grade with what became known as, "The Hairy Bottom Talk," but was officially known as "Growing and Changing". Here the boys and girls were separated into two rooms and told they would soon be growing hair around their private parts and given a deodorant. I am sure it went into a little more depth, but it basically was informing them how their bodies would change with very little explanation as to the why and its role in the continuation of our species.

The next discussion came in their Sophomore year of high

school, when the kids were 16, after the legal age of consent and way after they could get married according to Massachusetts law which abhorrently had no official minimum age if parental consent was granted. As my boys said it was way too late as most of the kids who were going to have sex had already had it.

Edward came home and informed us that they have started sex ed at school.

"Thank goodness for that," I said jokingly, "I thought you were going to have to learn it off your brothers, like your dad did!"

James signified his horror with the cries of "Oh surely not! You expected me to tell him all that? Dear God! Edward, I hope they told you that if you are going to have sex, don't be silly and just wrap your willy!"

"Yes, but not every time. They can't always get pregnant?" Edward replied.

Again the school seemed to have failed to reinforce not only that it only took once to get a girl pregnant, but that, 'wrapping your willy," did not just prevent pregnancy, but also STDs.

"Edward, I have had unprotected sex three times in my entire life," I pointed out holding my glance on each of my three children to bring home the message I was trying to give.

A terrified look came over his face as, "Oh" signifying his newly found realisation.

"You know condoms protect you against diseases too? James added, "You missed all that with Mr. Chadwick didn't you, because we moved back here?"

"I know about all the diseases. We got to feel a model!"

"What kind of model male or female?"

"Both"

Maybe America was a little more progressive than I thought, but I could not help but wonder what diseases had they discovered from "feeling a model" and if they had washed their hands thoroughly after this investigation?

"Did they mind? Did Everyone feel them? Who signs up for that job?"

"No mum they were made of rubber. Not live models! They showed us how to examine ourselves for boob and ball cancer."

America seemed to tell them far too little and far too late and focused on their own bodies, not their interactions with others, so we added a little chat on the diseases others may pass on to you and recreated Mr. Chadwick's lesson over the dinner table.

James, not only had the benefit of an international sex education, but also gained information from other sources. I first became concerned when his love of Greek history opened up a whole can of worms. His TV show on the lives of Greek gods started talking in detail about having sex with bulls and a quick google, to find out if the prefix bi and tri are of Latin or Greek origin, led to the discovery of a whole load of stuff a sheltered young boy should not even know was physically possible connected to Latin and bi!

This was nothing compared to the education provided by his new cell phone number when we returned to the States. It turned out that Greg, the previous owner of James's new number, liked Hooters, sold logs, supported the Patriots and needed to renew his insurance. The phone rang constantly, revealing why Greg had needed a new number thus making him less easy to trace. As Dominic and I climbed into bed on Christmas Eve, after arranging gifts in expectant stockings, we overheard James chatting in his room. It was now after midnight and he knew that electronics were forbidden after nine, so we went in to tell him this was unacceptable. His shocked and confused face alerted us to the fact that something was wrong. As he laid on his bed, his face illuminated by the dim light of the bedside lamp, Dennis his teddy bear sitting dutifully beside him, he was repeating, "I am sorry but.." The voice on the other end of the phone was not listening and was not interested in any "buts", it was just shouting at a terrified fourteen year old boy.

"Are you ok? We asked, taken aback by what seemed to be happening, as the deep male voice on the other end of the phone could be heard in a muffled tone.

"Just keep away from my wife you bastard or I will kill you!"

Abruptly the conversation ended as the caller slammed down the phone, assuming that his final warning was enough to make our child comply.

"He thought I was Greg," said James apologetically "He said Greg should go and have sexual intercourse with himself and not with the man's wife."

At first, we were unsure how to respond, but we decided not to call the guy back since explaining was not going to achieve anything and after giving our sweet little James a hug, left the accused adulterer to wait for Father Christmas.

I don't know if Greg had contracted one of the diseases covered by Mr. Chadwick, but it was not out of the question, since Greg was probably not entirely faithful. I began to wonder if I had made the wrong career choice when the nice lady texted Greg, (now James), to tell him her new rates for a wide range of sexual services for which the lowest hourly rate was ten times what I was earning as a teacher. Since I am assuming a master's degree is not essential for allowing gentlemen like Greg to "take you up the backwards bottom" I could not help, but wonder if my education was a barrier to my earning potential!

The lack of openness in America, regarding sex, did not mean that it did not exist or that prostitutes were not part of some peoples' lives. People still had affairs, still fancied other genders and their own gender and still had internal battles to grapple with over sexual orientation. I do think that the lack of openness just meant that they had fewer people to share those battles and concerns with and may have made them feel a sense of not belonging to the norm because the norm was defined by this silence.

This became part of my battle to belong too as I became more puritan, learning that my lack of a filter was detrimental and could lead to social suicide. When discussing the newly discovered addition to your three year old's vocabulary, it may be better to tell his preschool teacher that in England that word has an alternative inappropriate meaning, rather than informing her that "bugger means take it up the arse," where you come from. So many times I would say something in a more formal setting and the room would fall eerily silent, alerting me to my inappropriateness. Despite thinking, "Note to self for the future. Turn on filter before staff meeting so I don't mention blue whale vaginas when nobody is even thinking about sea mammal genitalia," I would often still blurt out something totally inappropriate to the point I began to feel like a liability.

However, as I got older I realised I am who I am. I have a wonderful family who is just honest and fun to be around. We are a strong unit who look after each other and love each other, quirky behaviour and all. Their education around sex was something I knew we needed to deal with at home, since I could not rely on the school, even for the basics. If I wanted my kids to go forth in their sexual journey fully prepared and for them to accept other people with differences in sexual preference and gender fluidity, I would need to instil this at home and not just expect them to absorb it by osmosis.

Growing up my mother's attitude to sex made most of the American parents I met seem genuinely liberal. Growing up sex had definitely been a taboo.
"Belly, Tits, Arse?" she yelled, her voice questioning both the contents and the grammar of the sentence.

"Yes, Grandma. Belly, Tits, Arse"

"It makes no sense and it definitely needs some commas."

James had not had an upbringing in which such sentences would bring shame to the speaker, so he felt comfortable asking his grandmother to edit his piece of work on a feminist poet. I had been shamed many times for sharing such words so, as "Belly, Tits, Arse," echoed out over skype, I just wanted to curl up in a ball. Somehow my mother seemed to accept this language from James, be it because it was not me she was talking to or because it was a piece of literature.

I don't know what shapes this moral code, deciding what is immoral and what is acceptable. Is it our culture, the historical beliefs and experiences of our forefathers, our generation, our peers, or our family, I suspect they all play a part, but based on James's conversation with his grandmother I doubt family plays a major role. Dominic's mother was the same generation and had the same culture as my mother yet she was much more open to such conversations even inviting Dominic, following her mastectomy, to feel both her breasts, one real and one fake.

Neither family typified the British approach to sex education, which had definitely changed from my time of get the basics in Biology lessons and the finer details in the hayfields during an awkward fumble. Now there was a PSHE (Personal, Social, Health and Economic education) curriculum which began in the younger years and covered all aspects of relationships, sexual and nonsexual, general health and wellbeing and promoted acceptance of other types of families, other than the traditional man and woman and children model. As they reach the age of eleven the subject of sexual relationships are explored in much more depth with some parts of the curriculum being compulsory for all children.

The British talked more openly about sex, but normally in

a jovial way, full of innuendo. Sex was something to be laughed at, brought up over a drink in the pub with a nod and a wink. Sex before marriage and same-sex relationships have become normalised and accepted, but infidelity would neither be accepted nor part of the humour. The Americans I met, on the whole, did not joke about sex in the same way and Germans saw it so much just part of life it did not seem to be in their humour either. This was a British thing.

Germany definitely proved to be a great source of sex education for the whole family. Germany sat firmly at the opposite extreme to America. Even on our trip to check it out as a country we discovered that Germany had a love of sex and the environment. Why waste petrol to go out and buy the whole family toys when you could kill two birds with one stone and pop into Toys R Us and the sex shop, who conveniently shared a car park and were right next door to one another. As we drove back to the hotel we went through the red light district passed what Dominic's colleague referred to as, the "special ladies". This was a strange term since they definitely did not seem anything special and some of them were not even ladies! Sex was not hidden. It was not taboo.

I picked up a packet of gummy sweets, strategically placed at the check out to tempt me. They looked delicious from the picture on the packet. Soft gummy discs, with what appeared to be a liquid centre and a fun character dancing on the packet, with a long sausage-shaped body and two, round, fat legs. As I climbed into the driver's seat of my little, red mini I decided to try one of the sweets from the bag that I had placed on the passenger seat next to me. I was going to share them with the boys when I got home, but I am greedy and wanted to get a couple to myself before I was forced to divide them between the four of us. As I pulled it out of the packet the tiny square silver foil in which it wrapped looked very familiar and the sweet inside was much flatter than I had imagined. As I ripped open the foil imagining the sweet fruity flavour and liquid centre running down my throat I realised that Billy Bobs were in fact condoms, not gummy sweets and the fun dancing character on the box was, in fact, a cock and balls winking at me as though to say, "Got you there!"

It really is no wonder that after living in Germany, a country where condoms in brightly decorated boxes were placed at the checkouts nestled in between the kinder eggs, Haribo, that my children talked very openly about sex. They had learnt that it was not taboo. The hairy bottom talk was given in preschool in Germany, not 5th grade when most kids had already got their sex education on the middle school bus. By the time a German student had reached 5th grade, they were well versed in what went where and were looking forward to moving on to placing Billy Bobs on Cucumbers during the lessons on contraception, discovering about mushrooms growing in vaginas in Mr. Chadwick's sexually transmitted disease unit or discovering interesting sexual practices involving a pineapple as they googled plant sex for Ms. Grafton's botany class! Although I was raised in the UK and had had a wider education than my mother's quick, "what went where" description, living in America for a while made me much more sensitive to shocking sexual content. On a trip home I was shocked to see how freely anal skin tags were shown on British TV and was even more shocked to be told by the same show to go online to check my boobs, balls and vulva. Directions to the latter two would have been useful if nothing else!

This openness was welcomed by me as a parent however. I had been too scared to approach my mother for advice. Germany made sex an open discussion and my children's willingness to bring it to the table and openly discuss worries made me feel less anxious and more confident that they would pursue their own sexual discoveries in safety.

It got to the point that I thought there was really nothing else that they could be taught and I was praying that we could have just one journey home from school that did not contain references to bull sperm, cows lady gardens, or whether or not its best to do it with a sausage or a straw! James had learnt about artificial insemination of cows in yet another of Mr. Chadwick's science classes and of course, he decided that the best place to share his newly found knowledge was in the car on the way home.

"So mum the bull puts his sperm in a straw and it is sent to the lady cow so that she can get pregnant"

"Ew!" said Edward "She has to drink sperm out of a straw?"

"No Edward it is inserted into her lady garden"

"Lady garden? What do you mean lady garden? That's ridiculous! Do you mean her vagina?"

"Vagina Vagina!" Henry repeated over and over in a sing-songy voice. "I love that word! Vagina Vagina!"

As he got out of the car he was still singing, "vagina vagina" as he skipped past the elderly neighbour doing her gardening. I hoped that the German word for vagina was not vagina, so we could maintain some degree of a relationship with the neighbours! However, German for vagina is indeed vagina, but luckily she was German and not my mother so just assumed that a young boy had been in the hairy bottoms class that day at Kindergarten.

Only a week went by when there was a feeling of de ja vu as Edward prepared for his science test the following day in the car on the way home, James asking him questions from the review sheet.

"Where are sperm made?"

"In your balls"

What is the proper name for those?"

"Uh your bits and bobs"

"No, try again"

"Your crown jewels"

"No"

"Meat and two veg? Well just in your two veg"
"No Edward its in your testicles!"
Henry then giggled uncontrollably as he repeated testicles over and over again for the rest of the journey. This resulted in a repetition of the vagina incident that led me to believe the neighbour did not actually need to work on her garden, but waited amongst the shrubs to see how the Gostick boys would embarrass their mother each day.

These euphemisms also seemed a British thing. America, in its puritan way, used biological terms and mentioned sex and private parts as little as possible, almost pretending that they did not exist. In Germany, it was so normal that they just said what needed to be said when and if it needed saying and had a practical utilitarian approach. As ever Britain was in transition from puritan to utilitarian, giggling its way through with the help of the odd lady garden filled with meat and two veg.

16 FEMINISTS DON'T APPROVE OF A TRAILING SPOUSE

The sexual revolution may be in full swing in the Gostick house, but I had somehow unknowingly taken a backward step in the feminist revolution, taking on the role of trailing spouse. I had a father and husband who respected women as their equals, but society's views did not. Feminism supposedly gives a woman a right to choose, but, in my experience, that only worked if you chose to rebel against the stereotypes. I didn't choose really. It just crept up on me and stole my independence and respect. From being a professional woman with assumed intellect, I became the trailing spouse with assumed fresh air for brains. I don't know if it was just my perception or if it was a reality, but soon I came to believe the assumptions and lost the confidence to return to my old life.

These feelings may have been shaped by attitudes to gender roles that shaped attitudes around me and I saw my boys developing some old fashioned views in response to what they saw in their communities. American families, in the suburbs like ours, tended to follow traditional roles much more than those in Britain and Germany with far more stay at home mums. This worried me in some aspects in that my boys started to accept the traditional roles as the norm.

James fit in perfectly with the uptight society, in which he had been raised, and revelled in the old fashioned dancing lessons that took part over a series of evenings in sixth grade in his Middle school.

The lessons were attended by almost all of the sixth grade and were seen as a right of passage. They were run by an elderly gentleman who ran a dance school and was a throwback to a much earlier time. His grey hair was brill creamed back and not single hair was out of place. He wore a navy blazer and cream trousers and enforced the traditional roles, encouraging girls to be submissive and boys to look after these delicate blooms like true gentlemen. I have no problem in my sons behaving like gentlemen, but I feel the general consideration for others, like holding a door open and not taking more than your fair share, are values that should be adopted by all. Boys were taught to have one handkerchief in their blazer's top pocket for show, one in their pocket for their own use and a third handkerchief in case the lady had a crisis. "One for show, one for blow and one for a lady's crisis." They were taught how to ask a lady to dance and buffet etiquette, which was not to load up your plate to overflowing and then gobble it all down as quickly as possible to get first chance at seconds. Henry was lucky enough to learn how to be a true gentleman too, but Edward, who would have possibly gained the most from such an education, missed the lessons because we were in Germany. He was, however, still under the illusion that he was landed gentry and the privileged lifestyle, in which he was raised, sat comfortably with him.

I followed the family rule that boys and girls needed to be prepared for all roles, no matter what the traditional assignment had been. Thus, James was learning how to cook and clean so he could leave home well prepared to look after himself. These were lessons they would all receive in varying intensity throughout their childhood.

Edward informed us that he would go to college in China and just employ a "cheap woman" to do it all for him.

Henry also seemed to be under the mistaken impression that women would run around after him too. One afternoon, when I told him to tidy his room, he informed me, in a self assured kind of a way, that, "You should do the tidying because you are a girl and girls wear skirts which they can use to carry all the stuff. That's why girls should always do the cleaning." He picked up the bottom of his T-shirt demonstrating the appropriate method and that his T-shirt did not have the capacity to hold a week's worth of debris and Thomas the Tank trains. "That's why they wear big skirts when they get married, so they have more skirt to tidy their stuff and their husbands!" he said.
"I will need a wife so she can do my washing while I watch the rugby because I won't be doing stuff like that," he added showing this was a well thought out theory. I passed him another train to add to the box which he dutifully dropped, creating a crash as it hit the plastic and the bottom of the once full container.
"Women are capable of doing more than just washing'.
"Yes I know." he explained, "You have the brains and dad has the muscles. That's why he plays rugby and you decide what things can be washed together!"
Once again I felt pride at his well-formulated theory and his affirmation that he intended to fight for women's rights when he grew up. I just hoped he knew that women wanted more than the right to do the washing.

I wonder if it was my decision to give up my career to look after them and become a trailing spouse that had given my sons these outdated ideas or if it was the community in which they were raised. It certainly was not the example of their father who was a firm believer in gender equality. It was hard for me to be seen, especially by my own children, as less successful than their father because of this choice. I felt that society, in general, saw me as less knowledgable and in some way lacking. Feminism does not always benefit women. Sometimes, it gives us the right to choose a career, but judges us for choosing a more traditional role. Whatever my boys' sexist statements may suggest they were raised to be self sufficient and not reliant on the help of a subservient woman.

James would later refer to my parenting style as "aggressive neglect". At first, these words had a negative connotation suggesting that as well as failing as a modern career woman, I had also failed as a 1950's caring mother, kissing her child off to school as she went back inside to spend the whole day dusting, scrubbing and cooking a perfect meal. James reassured me that this was not the case. He added that he thought this was a good approach because when he left home he was independent and competent, unlike those parented with the helicopter style. The aggression which apparently accompanied my neglect had caused my boys to develop their own warning system according to James:

Code red 1 - Clean up quick she is going to explode.

Code Red 2 - Too late she's exploded stand well clear.

Code red 3 - Do whatever she just said really quickly because we may get TV with chocolate. Indeed, when James compared me and Matilda and said "She just bites my hand off, but you bite my head off!"

My kids packed their own lunch from their first day of preschool to when they left at eighteen. They were expected to empty the dishwasher, clean their own rooms and help with the laundry. Even though we had cleaners, they never cleaned the kids' rooms because I believed that they should learn to be responsible for themselves. My hope was that this would mean they were better prepared for life when they left home.

My Dad's parents had employed a similar system, the boys learning to bake and the girls to fix their dad's coal wagon.

I too had been expected to learn the skills traditionally applied to both genders.

When Dominic's dad once stayed with us in America he was annoyed by a squeaky door.
"Where is Dominic's oil can?" he enquired intending to oil the hinges.
"He doesn't have one," I replied.
"Well, how would he oil this squeaky door?" he exclaimed in disbelief.
"He'd borrow mine!" I replied walking away and leaving him to endure the squeak a little longer. Again the sensible and easy route would just have been to give him "our' oil can, but again I never took the easy route and letting things go was just not in my nature.

As we all finished up a cup of tea and slice of cake, Dominic's father held his arm out straight with his plate balanced precariously on his open palm. This was my silent signally to remove his crockery and wash it. I should have just taken it into the kitchen. That is what I should have done. Instead, I found the need to make a stand. In an act of defiance, I reached over to his outstretched hand and placed my plate on top of his, the china making a tingling sound as one plate hit the other.
"Ah thanks," I said passively-aggressively implying that his behaviour was not acceptable. He leant forward and placed the plates on the table with a scowl, acknowledging my defiance and his disgust at my failure to know my place. Dominic's mum just gave a wry smile, secretly pleased, I think, that I had made a stand for our sex.

After reading Dominic's Gran's very old book on household management, I realised that these misogynistic ideas were nothing new. Apparently one must never have a kitchen less than 8ft in any direction, so as to allow both one's scullery maid and cook to move easily! The book also provided instructions to share with one's housekeeper on how to repair one's silk umbrella. Now I just need to move to China where apparently, according to Edward, there are plenty of women who fulfil these roles and presumably silk umbrellas to repair! If Dominic's father had been raised by a woman whose life was governed by such a book his attitudes would have been understandable, but Dominic's Gran was a progressive woman who always always wore the trousers so the source of his beliefs remained a mystery.

My dad would equally expect his plate to be taken in the kitchen for him, but he would ask in a way that made you feel like you were the most wonderful thing in his life. He would make you feel valued for your help rather than just expecting it.
"Just take this in the kitchen for me love will you?" he would ask and then, as you took the plate, he would smile and say, "Thanks. You're a good 'ne."

My mother was a woman who did not want to conform to her gender role, but she did and resented it. She went out to work and cooked and cleaned the house whilst, in the latter years of his life, also looking after my grandfather who now lived a couple of doors down. She had the worst of both worlds constrained by a traditional role, yet her time consumed with the pursuits of a modern woman. My dad was more than capable of helping with cooking and cleaning, but worked long hours and took on the demeanour of a helpless, yet grateful puppy.

Mine and Dominic's original plan was to move to the States for a couple of years before Edward started school, and then we would return home and I would take up where I left off. This would allow me , unlike my mother, to have the best of both worlds. My children and I were therefore thrust into this Stepford wives style environment. Somehow I found myself sat in coffee mornings talking about cleaning products and mind-numbing TV shows, any trace of my intellect ebbing away. A couple of years rolled into five and then ten, until the thought of up and leaving my Groundhog Day type of existence and moving to Germany, seemed a welcome relief to the monotony, but a new monotony awaited me. Now a new set of women, with new places to meet for coffee greeted me. Instead of British women, fresh off the boat, desperately searching for bacon, sausage and a jar of marmite, now I sat with American women in search of peanut butter, marshmallow fluff and hot dogs. I had nothing in common with these women. I wanted to try new foods, see new ways of doing things, hear new ideas. After all, that was why I was here, to escape the sameness of the everyday. I wanted to wander the streets with a lantern in October, not with Captain America shouting "Trick or treat" at the bemused locals. I wanted bratwurst, not hot dogs, electric cars, not petrol powered rainforest killers. I wanted to sit and talk about politics and science, not cleaning fluids and Desperate Housewives.

My German class brought me the relief I had been longing for. A room filled with people with different ideas, different foods, all looking to assimilate into a new land, but still keep their own identity. The classes pushed me to the limit intellectually. I wasn't the smartest person in the room and I needed to fight to keep up. I loved it! I was challenged and inspired, but at 12.30pm it all ended as I met up with the international mums for lunch, listening to complaints of education without a rubric and frustrations at German's who did not speak good enough English.

Special ed was virtually nonexistent at the school. An Italian school psychologist battled to help children with emotional problems as a result of being thrust into a school with an unfamiliar language and she tried her best to help my boys with accommodations for their dyslexia, but she was stretched painfully thin. I decided that I needed to be able to help them myself so, with my newly discovered confidence from learning German, I enrolled on a distance learning Master's degree in Special Education and Inclusion through Birmingham University. This allowed me to replace afternoons of mindless dribble, with shocks of new knowledge which resurrected my brain like bolts of electricity bringing Frankenstein's monster to life. The resulting creature was, to the coffee mums, indeed a monster. I was not available for shopping trips or campaigns to Americanise the PTA, and soon I became an outsider in the group to which I was meant to belong. Other women had shown independent thoughts and been ostracised before me, so I knew the drill, but it still made me feel alone. I didn't want to be one of them, yet I did. I didn't know where I fit in, which crate to reside in. My people were all professional working women. People who needed intellectual stimulation and found it through careers, but that was not an option for me. I found that stimulation through my degree and German classes, but I needed people to laugh about my failures and talk about new experiences and this group took me a while to find. You will kiss many frogs before you find a prince and the ex-pat coffee mums were the frog to me and kissing the frogs was tough, but eventually, I found the princes or should I say, princesses.

I worried that my battle to find a place in the world and my decision to semi occupy the world of the coffee mums impacted my boys' view of a woman's place. The women they saw were either mindless trailing spouses or over-sexualised TV stars and music princesses.

Edward's view, I worried, was shaped by the latter. In Build a Bear he asked if he could get a pole because his teddy wanted to try pole dancing and become a stripper. James came to my rescue and sorted out my inability to find a response by telling him that Spencer Bear had no private parts and only wore a scarf anyway, so probably had limited career prospects in the sex industry. As Bruno asked Edward on the way to scouts if he knew how to tie a clove hitch he replied, "Sure I have a great way to remember you just imagine the two ends of the ropes are a woman's legs then you just push the…" I stopped the conversation right there! He had grown up in a world that had school trips to brothels and 3D peep shows and drove past the "Special ladies" when we picked his dad up from work, before stopping off that the Toys R Us sex shop duplex for some lego. All this seemed to have given him a realisation of the pleasures of the female form a little earlier than I would have liked!

James on the other hand seemed to be more influenced by the coffee mums, seeing women as creatures to be respected and protected. He offered advice to his brothers on treating women well, and saw himself as a gentleman. In a play area filled with brightly coloured plastic spheres, Henry waited patiently at the top of a slide as a little girl sat, legs dangling down the blue plastic towards the ball pit below. She was refusing to either launch herself down the slide or move aside and let the other children take a turn. Her American mother who had crawled through a series of tubes after her offspring to offer the full helicopter parent approach said in a soft encouraging voice, "Please move Emily we need to share. This little boy would like a turn." Emily sat indignantly knowing that the consequence of her inertia would be frankly, nothing. At this point, a German mother would have yelled a "Das Geht Nicht" or two and pushed their stubborn offspring firmly down the slide, but Henry knew that was never going to happen so took matters into his own hands. He decided to use of biological warfare. As he picked his nose and wiped it in her hair. A look of horror came over the mother's face as she scooped little Emily up and allowed Henry instant access to the slide. James who had been looking on from below, horrified at his younger sibling's ungentlemanly behaviour, advised him that he would never impress a woman by wiping bogies on them and that he may need to try an alternative approach. Later that day, as Henry came down the giant slide in the very busy play area, naked, even James realised he was a lost cause as explained that his trousers and underwear made the slide "too slippy!"

Edward was also given lessons on relationships by James and when he told us that a girl at school was really annoying, James told him that when he was older he would realise that the annoying ones are the ones you end up marrying! At times they would work together to try and understand the fairer sex, but as for all men, women would remain a mystery. When I asked Edward what he thought we should buy a girl in his class for her birthday party he decided to consult his brothers.
"What does she like?"
"Well, she likes bacon so we could get her bacon". Henry then joined in and explained there had to be another way to please a girl that didn't involve bacon. All three boys thought long and hard and all concluded that if you want to impress a woman it had to be bacon! I, at this point, feared I may never have a daughter in law!

Edward soon came to the conclusion that he did not need his big brother's advice as he had it all worked out for himself. Indeed, he was the one the girls all had a bit of a thing for. He was long and skinny with protruding ears and a crazy mop of red hair. Not normally every girl's dream, but he had charisma. Lots of Charisma! He knew how to manipulate people into falling in love with him, but it took him a while to refine the finer details.
"I'm glad I had a bath because now I smell nice and Gavin says that's what I have to do to get a girlfriend. He's going to help me get one because he has three!"
I asked what else Gavin had advised. "Well," he said, "You have to smell nice, have good breath, tell them they look pretty and not do anything disgusting unless they are holding a worm and then you can be really disgusting because they'll like it!"

Edward then disappeared off into his room and yelled across the hall, "Can you smell my aftershave? Have I got enough on and when can Colby come for a playdate?"
Colby was going to be one lucky girl as long as she stays away from worms that's all I can say!

He knew what were his positive assets and told his friend Toby that they didn't need to worry because they wouldn't struggle to get girlfriends.
"They go for the accent you know." Toby said that he thought that they also went for personality, but Edward reassured him that they had the accent and the personality so were all set!

As a great romantic visiting the beautiful city of Venice Edward informed us that he had always intended proposing to this lucky lady there, but since he had seen the prices here he probably wouldn't bother. He also had a plan to buy her a ring a couple of sizes bigger than she needed because, "They all get fat once you marry 'em." The expensive nature of marriage was not his only limiting factor as he informed us that, "at some point you have to decide whether you want a wife or a urinal because you can't have both".

Dominic had always treated me as an equal and my own father had not totally conformed to gender roles, again. I wondered, as I watched my own boys navigate the road to understanding the fairer sex, what it was that shaped your future relationships. It seemed, looking at Dominic and my father, not to be based on your own father's attitudes. Both my Grandmother and Dominic's mum were strong independent women who manipulated misogynistic husbands, so maybe it was your mother who shaped your attitudes to women. In which case what lesson was I teaching them? Was I setting them up for success in their future relationships?

All the boys were quite open about their plans for the future, when they became real men, and James and Edward discussed at which point this would happen. James suggested it was when you go through puberty to which Edward replied, "No its when you loose your, oh er what do you call it mum? When you lose your?"
I was just about to help him out with "virginity?" when he added, "When you lose your last baby tooth!" He obviously did not fully understand the word virginity because on another occasion informed us that James had lost his virginity whilst in the kitchen making a cup of tea and I realised there may be a need for another little chat!

Henry said he wanted to live with me forever, as he snuggled up next to me, but then he clarified that this meant that when I died he'd get the house and all our money and he'd be rich. He was always my most affectionate child. The only way to get a hug from James was to put all his electronics on one side of me and him on the other and as he reached over me, imagining it was a hug, but Henry's were freely offered. I remember him getting out of the pool and asking for a cuddle during his swimming lesson. When I told him that I couldn't cuddle him until after his lesson, I watched him purposely bang his head on the step then run back to me and say, "I hurt myself now you have to cuddle me." A bit extreme but he just loved cuddles! When Dominic was away and Henry was still in preschool, it was a real treat for him to sleep in my bed and watch a documentary on TV, usually about space. He was a nightmare to sleep with and moved around all night. I often wondered what he dreamt about, but when one morning his first words after waking were, "Have I still got a Batman tattoo on my bum?" I had a much better idea.

My life was never boring. The cacophony of shrieks that would fill the house were never predictable. This unpredictability made life a mix of fun surprises and made the people who mattered to us love our family for the unfiltered band that they were. We soon learnt to value those relationships that mattered and reject the toxic people. It is not a love of the British accent or the ability to give unlimited cuddles that brings strength to relationships, but valuing the people within that relationship and accepting their individualities unconditionally. Most of my joy is generated within the four walls of our home and most of the stresses come from beyond those walls. I hope my boys have the same situation so that there is always a safe space to retreat to and partners who enrich their lives. I think my time in Germany reinforced my belief that life is short so, do not take time away from the people who enrich your life to spend it with those who don't. I was never going to feel comfortable with the coffee mums so being ostracised was their gift to me. It allowed me to discover like minded individuals. I realised I will never conform to any individual crate and I was fine with that. I am a feminist who loves to be a homemaker, but has no interest in cleaning. I am a British woman in an international world. I need other accepting nonconformers and nothing less will do. I hope our time in Germany taught my boys these lessons too so that they find gentle fruits to share their baskets with and have the confidence to reject the familiar.

17 SEEING THE BEAUTY IN OTHER CRATES AND BASKETS

We are all preprogrammed to crave a feeling of belonging. Belonging to a tribe gave our ancestors the security of numbers, it increased your chance of survival and passing on your genes to the next generation. In the end, we all want to be accepted, to fit in. It's hard when you move from one culture to another. What is it though that makes us belong, that makes us part of a tribe? Is it the place we were born, the place I left or is it the place we inhabit, the community I chose to be a part of rather than it being assigned to me by birth and DNA?, I would argue it is neither.

High on the moorland of the Pennines governments decided to change boundaries in the early 70s. Homes that had once proudly displayed the red rose of Lancashire were now magically sitting in villages whose signs bore the white rose of Yorkshire. Within hours the white roses had been daubed with red paint showing the communities displeasure at being reassigned to the opposing tribe. They all lived in the same place as the day before. Their place had not changed only the name of the county in which it sat. This shows that it is more than just the physical place to some extent. It is the perception of that place and the inhabitants' acceptance or not of that perception.

Preston Guild was a chance to belong. Like Mary and Joseph returning to Bethlehem to be counted, all Prestonians feel a calling, every 20 years, from their home town and flock back like swallows in the springtime. The Guild celebrations first came about in 1179 after King Henry II awarded Preston with its first royal charter, along with the right to have a Guild Merchant. Traders, craftsmen and merchants, belonging to a guild were the only people allowed to trade in the town and must swear loyalty to the Mayor and the Guild Merchant in a public court where their credentials were checked and they paid a small fee. Soon gatherings for renewing membership became infrequent and from 1542, Preston Guild took place every 20 years, allowing for renewal once in a generation. In 1790 the need to be part of a guild was no longer applicable as the town became a free trade town, but the parties, processions and festivities that had accompanied this once in a generation gathering continued. Still every twenty years Prestonians returned to the place of their birth to renew their sense of belonging. At this time, it did not seem to matter that I had chosen another place to call my home. All that was important was that I was born there and cared enough to continue the tradition and return. As people chatted in the streets, I was one of them and my adventures were something for the town to be proud of. I felt secure and safe. Here it was my crate that mattered not the hodgepodge of returning fruits, each with a little melon DNA, but reshaped by differing experiences. This was not the norm though.

You even find that your own people no longer accept you as being a part of their crate. You become so squashed out of shape that you are no longer recognised as from your own place, but your original form eliminates you from any other. At any other time other than the Guild my acceptance to the tribe had other requirements and I felt an uneasy anxiety that I may be rejected at any time for a misplaced word which revealed my betrayal.

One time, when I went back home we were in Centre Parcs. This was a holiday oasis for busy families just wanting a safe place to unwind. Hidden amongst the towering pines were log cabins each with a place to park a bike, but not a car. The gate opened only on Mondays and Fridays when refreshed families packed up cars which had sat in a distant car park, whilst exhausted groups arrived unloading their cars into the wooden sanctuaries before returning them to the car park and picking up bikes. Children wandered the roads and paths within the outer walls with the freedom I had experienced as a child, with only a rumbling stomach or newly illuminated street light to signal it was time to go back for supper. In the centre was a huge dome in which an enormous water park sat, free to everyone during their stay. Of course, Starbucks had found its way into this uncommercial paradise chipping away at the facade of yesteryear. Starbucks was not a thing when we left England, but now their double cupped paper disposable wares were in every town jostling for superiority with Costa and treading on the old fashioned tea rooms with china cups and saucers that reminded me of home. After a trip to the little shop next to the Centre Parcs Starbucks, I popped in for a quick cup of tea and stood in line to request my, "Awake tea please," as I had so many times in Southborough
"You what love? What's that?"
"It's like English breakfast"
"Well, why did yer not ask for English Breakfast or even just tea mi duck?

I had now been conditioned by my new found culture that tea came in a variety of flavours, including fruits, and that this array may even be presented to me from the dreaded box of stale teas that sat in the back of restaurants, year on year waiting for some strange alien to request one of the paper packages. I had become accustomed, although had never accepted, the cup of lukewarm water in which I was supposed to desperately try to extract some flavour from the American bag in the paper package, if I had managed to find some real tea rather than some herbal substitute that is.

In England, nobody asks for awake tea. It isn't even called that. English Starbucks labels it English Breakfast, but the servers all know you will just call it tea because nobody drinks anything other than English Breakfast. This signalled to them that I was not one of them anymore, but I sounded like them so I must just be pretentious. It was worse than not being accepted. It was like I had chosen to make myself above them and this was why I would need to be rejected. I felt deflated. My shoulders dropped and my day lost the energy it had had before I walked into an American franchise to be made to feel unBritish. I got on my bike and started to peddle back feeling alienated. The lack of cars on the roads made it hard to remember which side of the road I should be on, cementing my feeling of not belonging. As I peddled down what seemed like the right side, a Centre Parcs van was heading straight for me. I tried to think hard and quickly as to which side I should be on and started to panic.
"I don't know what side of the road I should be on!" I yelled out, to anyone who would listen, my voice shaking.
"Same side as normal love!" came the reply from a family walking down the lane feeling normal. I wasn't feeling any sense of normal. I had no normal. Half of my life driving on the left was normal and then all of a sudden driving on the right was normal. One minute "awake" was normal and then just "tea" was normal. If I did not know my own normal, how could anyone else be expected to see me as normal, as part of their crate? When my school friend came to visit with her children her son would start every sentence with, "well in our country". That was my country, my country long before it was his, but he saw me as foreign, unfamiliar, not normal for his country. Normal for

160

me was fish paste sandwiches for school, but for my children, lobster was a more familiar sandwich filling, lobster the food of the rich that you saw on the movies, not for a Lancashire lass!   As we stuffed tights with newspaper and made an effigy of a 16th century terrorist and slumped him next to the fridge waiting to be burnt for Bonfire Night, Henry referred to him as mummy's friend. He was indeed my friend, a memory of bonfire nights gone by where burning effigies of Catholics was normal for the whole town, catholic and protestant alike. When I rang the Fire Department and told them what we were about to do, so that it would not be misconstrued as a real fire, they saw it as far from normal and were quite concerned about our heretic like behaviour.

Knowing where to belong and what was normal was a battle for my children too when they were required to define themselves by place. Despite Henry's observation that he could not be English because he didn't talk weird, nationality comes down to more than just your accent or even where you were born. My children did not know where they were from, an alien concept to most other parents, but a familiar one for families who have chosen to roam the planet.   Henry told his teacher that he was born in America, but made in Jamaica, with British parts. A truly international child providing a little more information than I think she wanted to know! Luckily for her however, when he needed a little clarification he came to us.
"How did Dad take an egg to Jamaica?"
Despite this accurate depiction of all the countries involved in his conception, he still did not know where he belonged, which crate was his. He cheered for Britain and America in the Olympics and was delighted when Usane Bolt brought medals back for Jamaica. At times he would sway more to one country than the other in a bid to belong with his peers. Pointing at the flag on his socks he asked whose flag it was
"That's your flag." I said "The British flag"

"Trust me dude it's not. My flag is the best flag, the Stars and Stripes."

At other times he would be British through and through as he searched for his own identity and the things that made him special. He once told me he felt most German because that was where he had been his happiest. I think for all of us the question "Where are you from?" had no answer.

This was demonstrated at the Pantomime in Preston Guildhall more than at any other time. Pantomime is a British thing that identifies you as in the tribe or out, through a secret code taught surreptitiously to children every Christmas. Not being privy to the code leaves you vulnerable and this unease was obviously felt by poor little Henry.

"I don't like it I want to go home. That woman is really a man and he's wearing a dress. It's just not normal!" I don't believe this was a reflection on his attitude to transgender rights, but more a feeling of things not fitting his cultural norms. He was correct that in pantomime many of the men are dressed as extreme caricatures of women, with large wigs and badly applied garish makeup, enormous fake bosoms protruding from brightly coloured dresses under which, enormous bloomers lurked waiting to be revealed in a dance number or unfortunate accident. The principal boy is always played by a thin woman in tights and high boots, who would slap her thigh and give a pert one-liner. Audience participation is essential to the plot and it is innate in any Brit to know when to shout, "He's behind you" or "oh no he doesn't!" If you are not born into this culture it is like being not in on the joke, not part of the group. One of the actors always calls children onto the stage and, out of all the hundreds of children in the audience, he decided to pick Henry as one of the four children to join the performance.

"Hello, What is your name and where are you from?"

"Sam and I'm from Longridge"

162

"Are you enjoying the performance, Sam?"
Sam nodded.
"Have you brought your sheep with you today?"
"No I haven't got a sheep," said Sam confused
"I thought everyone in Longridge had sheep aren't you all farmers there and very well acquainted with your sheep?"
The audience laughed at the innuendo that went right over Sam's head.
"How about you young lady? Where are you from and what is your name?"
"Sophie. I'm from Ribchester"
"Oh, we have the posh crowd in tonight Ladies and Gentlemen. Sophie is from Ribchester so we all be on our best behaviour.
"How about you pal? Where are you from and what is your name?"
"Henry. Er I am from er oh I am from The world!" he spluttered

The audience burst into laughter, expecting to hear a village on the outskirts of Preston, but instead being given a planet. For Henry though, this was the only answer he could give. He did not have one place in which to belong he had several places. His sense of self was not defined by place, but by other factors. I think the fact that I felt a sense of belonging at Preston Guild, but not in Centre Parcs shows that it was something other than the physical place which made me feel comfortable with my environment. Therefore, one must ask if it is the people that make you feel a sense of belonging? Is it people who were born or raised where you were or is it a characteristic that you share? Is that characteristic physical or is it an attitude, a behaviour or a set of values?

Whatever it was, we knew that we would never belong anywhere completely again, but when we were with certain friends we didn't have to worry about sounding disloyal, pretentious or out of place, because they just got it. What was it about these friends that invoked those feelings of acceptance? It wasn't with all the people we spent time with, but maybe those who did not bring this feeling should be described as acquaintances, not friends. This would suggest that belonging is reliant on the people you share a place with but that it is something specific about those people, a gift that not everyone chooses to give.

In Edward's class of twelve children in Germany, there were eleven different nationalities and six different religions, but they played together, celebrated each other's cultures and religious celebrations and ate each other's food swapping the contents of school prepared lunches that had been assembled with no regard for religious differences, almost always containing a pork product. Everyone belonged, nobody was other because they all had come from elsewhere. This is what bound them all together. It sparked an interest in differences, not condemnation. The polite, Japanese boy soon learnt not to wait to be served when sitting at an American table or else he would starve and in turn, the American children learnt to roll their own sushi.

One of these classmates was Edward's friend Ramiro, the son of a German mother and a Cuban father. He lived in a house at the end of his grandparents' garden with his mother for half the year and in the same house with his mother and an eleven piece Cuban band for the rest of the year. His father,Gilberto, played the double bass and was a laid back man with gentle big brown eyes and a gypsy lifestyle. Ramiro's mother Michelle was a highly strung University professor who also acted as the band's manager whilst they were in Germany. When I say she was highly strung this should not be taken as a criticism. It was a necessity to bring order to her world and that of Ramiro. She tolerated a band in her house and a husband who came and went. She fought with a school that rarely had the pupils' interests at heart and she was one of the kindest people I met during my time in Deutschland. She would ask us over for a barbecue in her garden and was again a multi-talented woman seeming to be a high performer in the world of academia, but also an accomplished bricklayer and builder having built her own house with the help of her father. On top of all of this she was also an excellent cook.

The evenings we spent at her house were the best times we spent in Germany. I felt like I belonged there. Laurie would often be there too with her children and it felt like our basket was in harmony. If Michelle were a fruit in that basket she should be a lychee, a tough exterior with a few spikes, but a sweet and rewarding middle that added an exotic mystery to the surrounding fruits. On one of these nights as the barbecue was loaded high with meats to feed the band, their girlfriends, Laurie's family and mine, I realised how lucky I was to experience all of these cultures in one. Bembels overflowed with juices and punches and the Cuban rum never seemed to dry up. As midnight struck the party began to get into full swing and instruments were pulled out of cases and the singing began. The tiny paved area between Michelle's house and that of her parents was hemmed in on all sides by other houses and sound of guitars and a double bass echoed off their walls. Nobody came out to complain as the sweet sounds of Latin music filled the humid air and smiles drew people for distant lands together in a celebration of humanity. Any stress flowed away on the string of notes and my shoulders fell as I sank into my chair and felt the cool fruit juice run down my throat as I sipped out of the Apfelwein glass. The kids swayed to the music and we all felt we had found our place. Michelle had not left the town in which she was born, but she had opened herself to every aspect of many other cultures and given some of her shared wisdom to us and this is what made me feel relaxed and understood and accepted. So often in Germany, especially in the school, I was always on my guard as to how my actions or comments may be judged. I rarely felt relaxed. I realised that night that it was not the shared experience of living in a foreign land that makes you feel accepted. Michelle was living in her native land, so it must be something more.

I was often among other ex-pats, but many of them wanted to change their surroundings into their familiar. This made me feel uncomfortable. If only their familiar crate was acceptable where did my crate fit in, where did the basket belong. Therefore it is not that shared experience of leaving your own land for another that makes you feel that you belong around someone. More it is the willingness of others to experience other cultures and not only take a little from them, but also give a little of themselves, that cultivates a sense of belonging. It is the ability to see the beauty in the different colours and shapes of haphazard fruits nestled together in a basket that is important, even if you are looking at that basket from within the plastic boundaries of your own crate of familiar fruits. You do not need to leave that crate to appreciate the beauty and likewise, you can have left your familiar crate and still be unable to see the exquisite nature of variability, instead of choosing to fight to rebuild the familiar plastic sides which constrain you. Michelle saw the beauty of the tropical basket, she added to it. She opened others' eyes to it. These made her the kind of person who made your shoulders sink into a chair as the stresses drained away and the beauty overwhelmed you.

Sometimes it was not just our culture that made us different, but also our physical appearance. Henry had once asked "Why have none of our family got normal coloured hair. Is it so you can find us in the pool?" He was right we always stood out in a crowd with such extreme hair, two redheads and a white blonde were never going to just blend. However, in an attempt to amalgamate into our surroundings, we headed to Breda in the Netherlands in

September of 2014. The boys thought it was just another random trip to a random place and climbed in the car for another few hours of the dog panting and dribbling over their shoulder. We sat in a cafe and had dinner and none of them noticed. We wandered the streets and explored the town and none of them noticed. We sat outside a bar and got a drink and Edward started to chat with a man on the table next to us from Germany. He had a long red beard and wild auburn hair flowing on to his violet T-shirt from beneath a black bandana tied tightly over his head. The lady next to him, who we later discovered was from France, wore a vivid purple T-shirt and flicked her long hair over her shoulders so that the flame-coloured locks glinted in the sun. She laughed and drank beer with the two Scottish brothers, both in lilac checked shirts who sat next to them and looked like James and Edward in 15 years time.

"Do you all know each other?" Edward asked in his normal confident way.

"No. We just met last night," one of the Scottish brothers replied.

Another man soon joined them carrying the next round of drinks, a sticker on his purple sweater showing he was Dutch, and as he sat down he removed his flat cap to reveal his ginger curls. Edward noticed the similarity with this international bunch, all wearing purple and all looking just like him. Suddenly he belonged. He was not the only ginger in the room. Eventually, the penny dropped with all of the family and it was the start of a fantastic weekend with our fellow 1614 gingers and a great, huge, ginger family atmosphere at the Breda Red Hair Festival. A very surreal weekend!

So as not to be left out I made Henry a t-shirt that said, "I just want to be ginger." He was soon spotted by a French TV channel who interviewed him on how it felt to not be a ginger in a ginger family and if he truly did just want to be ginger. Here, there were people from all over the world, black, white, but mostly very very white, united in their gingerness. It was as though everyone knew each other, chatting and buying rounds of drinks, helping each other with clues on the ginger scavenger hunt and all squeezing in together for a big family photo for the Guinness Book of World Records.

Maybe all you need to feel you belong is one striking thing in common even if that is just your ginger hair. Like Preston Guild for a small window in time, all you needed to unite you with those around you was one thing in common. I wonder if that time was extended, if flaming locks would be enough to maintain that sense of belonging. I suspect not. I think it needs the ability to see the beauty in unlike characteristics that brings with it a feeling of acceptance, not a need to be around those who mirror your own attributes.

Experiencing other ways of thinking does not make you wiser or stronger, it is accepting those differences that allows you to grow. Before I left the borders of Lancashire for the distant lands of Wales, I had a set of ideals that had never been questioned. Lancashire was the greatest place on earth. Perhaps the fact that less than 50% of Americans even have a passport, is why so many feel the need to exclaim with confidence that theirs is the greatest country on earth. This for many is not just a phrase giving a vague ideal, but is a firmly held belief based on the view from their own backyard. If they were to leave their immediate surroundings they would discover other places with better infrastructure, better education systems and better healthcare. I would argue they would struggle to find a place with better seafood or steaks, but that is the point. Every place has something to offer, something they excel at. There is no one place that is the greatest or the best, but each has something it can teach us. In my search for a place to belong, I learnt that despite having the best cheese and the obscure traditions I loved, Lancashire was not the greatest. I learnt that my greatest may not be your greatest and that was ok. As someone who is opinionated and unfiltered and who suffers for this, I learnt that sometimes it is better to be quiet than right. Forcing your culture and beliefs on to others will not bring you happiness or them enlightenment. They may like their plastic crate and who am I to force them into my basket. It may be correct that the basket is the greatest the best place to be, but I don't need to share this. It is better to remain silent than to be right. When I tried to indoctrinate the coffee moms, who had come to Germany as trailing spouses, with the benefits of European education or squash their taboos, allowing them to relax, I may have been right, but I was never going to change their opinions which they believed to be correct. This was what I took away from my time in Germany. In order to feel a sense of belonging, find those who see the beauty in differences, that is not always easy to do, and when you find them treasure these rare specimens and value their insight. At all other, times learn when to be silent and when to be right and expect to spend many more hours in silence than exactitude. This brought me more peace and contentment than I could ever have hoped for and meant it was easier to belong and be accepted. Sometimes your sense of belonging is a facade brought about by your silence, but should not replace the true contentment brought about by sharing the beauty with like-minded souls.

18 BYE BYE TO ALL MY WORLDLY GOODS HOPE TO SEE YOU AGAIN

Eventually, the time came for us to leave Germany and return home to America. As with everything else in Germany, there were procedures to be followed and rules to be obeyed, all with little regard for common sense. It was only a few months earlier that we suddenly realised that we had not had any post delivered and when I asked the postman, he explained that, since the sun had faded our name on the mailbox, he could no longer deliver our mail, despite waving to me every morning and peddling as fast as he could to avoid a barking Matilda. This was the German way. If the rules say you cannot deliver mail unless there is a readable name on the mailbox then, despite feeling able to read the name the previous day, if you decide it is no longer readable then you will no longer deliver the mail. You don't think to mention it to the homeowner as you shout, "Guten Morgen" or just use a little common sense and figure out that the homeowner has not changed. Germany was such a country of contradictions and although I would not miss the rule following I would miss the rebels who showed a total disregard for the unspoken rules that was exemplified by a middle aged man we spotted in speedos on a flowery bikes cycling through the city on our last trip into Frankfurt!

Germany had given us so many surprises and life was

never boring, whereas in America everything was so predictable from the North Face black coats every blond Stepford wife wore from October to April, to the predetermined sports the kids played in each of the seasons.

After a party or two arranged to wish us good luck on our way and a few days of men packing boxes and covering furniture in bubble wrap, the container that would take our things back across the ocean arrived. Permits had been obtained and the neighbours had been informed that they could not park on the adjoining road between certain hours, so that the lorry and container could access our street. The removal men who had been packing up our boxes started to load all our belongings into the container which had arrived early that morning. The driver of the lorry on which the container sat, however, just sat in his cab all day and listened to his radio and read his newspaper. His job was to drive, so he did nothing else. This was his job and that was the job he would do. He ate the pizza we ordered to feed the workers. Listening to the radio is hungry work! Matilda made the pizza delivery man work for his money. She was well and truly fed up of her day being disturbed by men carrying boxes, so when he arrived it was the last straw for her. She barked and chased him down the street, but we were ok because he dropped the pizza before he ran for his life.

Eventually all our worldly goods were squeezed into the container, and it was time for him to get on his way to the port. As he snoozed in his cab though he had not noticed a neighbour parking his car at the end of the road which ran perpendicular to the only way out of ours. He hadn't seen the neighbour choose to wander off away from his house into the distance. He hadn't therefore made sure that there was nothing blocking the end of our road and his ability to be on his way. This was the only thing he had to do all day and this was the only thing he hadn't done.

As the time ticked by it became too late for him to legally drive away, so he asked us to sign a paper that said we would pay for the hours he slept in his cab overnight. We had already paid for the hours he had been sleeping all day whilst everyone else worked like dogs, trying to load the container in time. The removal men, who were well and truly fed up of him by now, told us not to sign because it was his fault that the road had become blocked and he should have stopped cars parking there. There was a lot of shouting between him and them, calls to the removal company which reinforced the workers opinion that we must not sign and then a bit more shouting. Finally, the driver shouted that he would block the street for the night and when he set off in the morning he would drive to a lay-by and empty out all we owned by the side of the road. I was a little worried as we all settled down for the night in the nearby horse farm and B&B. I suppose I should have been terrified, but by now this was my third international move and I expected at least some breakages. You leant to expect the unexpected.

When the skies turn green and the phone echoes out the siren, warning of a tornado, you have minutes to decided what is your most precious possession to grab and take in the basement with you. Moving continents was no different. Warnings of containers being dropped into the sea resulted in the boys scrapbooks, photos and mementos being added to the safety of our hand luggage and air freight. These were the things that could not be replaced. Our gypsy lifestyle made you value memories as you discovered palpable possessions were expendable, often being left in storage for years on end. Memories bound our family unit together, shaped our perception of the world and altered our values. In short memories are what make us who we are. Photos and scrapbooks and childhood drawings rekindled those memories.

One such treasured possession was a letter that my dad

had written to me in my pre reg year in Bristol because, when I read it, it felt like I was listening to his voice. Its dry humour felt like a tight hug from my father, accompanied my a gentle rub of my back that told me I was his treasured possession. He apologised for being a bit cranky which I never remember him being, but blamed this on fatigue, "Due to some idiot half blinding me the day before" and the "lack of stimulants namely salt and sugar" His love of sweet tea meant that sugar was consumed by the pound and his letter explained that northern men, like himself, liked their tea like their women sweet and strong. My dad showed his love with insults, always accompanied by a wry smile. I was the idiot who had half blinded him, the owner of the big bum who had broken the toilet seat he fixed, and the person who failed to load his food in salt and drinks with sugar. It was now fifteen years since my dad had left us, his aorta rotted by sugar and salt and I missed him as much as ever. The letter was a piece of him that remained, so I treasured it and kept it back to put in my hand luggage on the plane. As we prepared to leave the house for the final time though I could not find it anywhere. I knew it was not in the container and that it was in the house, but the house was empty. I was devastated! I had lost my father's voice. I could deal with the possibility of everything in the container being strewn along the autobahn from Frankfurt to Hamburg, but I could not cope with this sheet of paper covered in my father's sprawling handwritten complaints being lost in the void of an international move. I felt sick as the panic built up in my stomach. I searched and searched even though the empty house had no places to hide. At that moment nothing mattered to me more, not the 6500 Euros we would loose if the house was not pristine, not the friends waiting to throw a goodbye party, not the need to organise the final details of getting the family home. Dominic loved me, as my father had, and always put my needs above his own. He was not annoyed by my obsession and helped with the search putting everything else to one side. He handed me the letter. He had found it on a high windowsill in the dark laundry room in the basement and finally I could breathe out again.

Clothes were essential in the short term so had been added to our airfreight and carry on, but I had not considered the clothes, James had now grown out of, as treasured possessions or short term essentials, so they were added to the container. However, since we were in the year in which Edward was to grow seven and a half inches, I had more need of the next size up trousers than I had of a scrapbook. His trousers were so short that James kept shouting "Run Forest run!" whenever he ran past.

The contents of our container therefore were expendable, even the old clothes, and not worthy of our worries. Based on the fact it seemed too much effort to even lift all of the food and the coffee to his mouth that we had given him the previous day it seemed unlikely that the lorry driver would single handedly empty out a container so I knew he was unlikely to leave all our stuff on the side of the road, but it was a relief when we finally saw it all again a few months later.

Once the house was empty we needed to repaint the whole thing to avoid loosing our deposit before an inspection from the letting agent, Herr Sommer. Our relocation agent suggested a Polish guy to help us with painting the high walls, we could not reach, and we did the rest. Like everyone in Germany, the painter was insistent that his work must be immaculate and we needed two or ideally three coats everywhere. We tried to explain it just needed to get us through the inspection, so one coat would be fine, but he was quite insistent so we compromised on two coats and tolerated a couple of days of disgruntled sighing and tutting before we handed over a bundle of Euros for his trouble. Herr Sommer arrived in his oversized jeep and headed towards us, his large gold medallion glinting in the summer sun against his hairy chest. Herr Sommer was probably in his 70s, but looked more like he was living in the 70s. He tried to hide his age with a large amount of jet back hair dye, which coated his shoulder length hair and he wore tight trousers and a heavily patterned psychedelic shirt unbuttoned almost to his waist. He was very excited to inspect the house, as he told us he had just had a row with our landlord and had no intention of helping "the tight bastard." I couldn't help, but wish that he had told us this before we had spent time and money painting the whole house, but I was still relieved as I stood nodding in agreement, my foot placed firmly on the chip in the laminate floor that had been made when my chair collapsed following the shaky journey across the Atlantic when we first moved in. As he wandered around he pointed out the things he would have put in his report if he didn't hate the landlord and confirmed we had passed the inspection with no problems being highlighted. This is virtually unheard of in Germany so we were excited to get most of our three month rent deposit returned as we were almost ready to close another chapter in our Romany story.

19 RETURNING THE ADVENTURE CHARIOT

Handing your final bags of trash over to the town you are leaving is the last interaction with the place who has given you stories, memories and new friends, before you give yourself to a new location. It is almost as though those bags contain the final stresses of daily life and as the town collects them, your worries are thrown into the truck with the old packaging and food scraps, empty paint cans and old toilet brushes and the transition from resident to visitor is complete.

The bin men came every two weeks and we would have left before they came so I needed to get rid of any trash to avoid losing our deposit. I drove with a bin bag full of old pizza, tea bags and leftover food from the freezer, threw it into the dumpster for non-recyclable trash and headed down the steps to my little red mini. The man from the dump followed me carrying my bag that he had retrieved from the dumpster. As always the German authorities resisted relieving me of my stress and he took his role as arsehole very seriously, as he emptied the contents of the bin bag onto the tarmac next to my car. He told me that household waste must be given to the bin men not placed in the dumpster. I explained my predicament, but sympathy is not something German officials have any familiarity with. With a quick reference to his similarities to his ancestors during the war, I got in my car and drove away, leaving him to scrape up my baked beans and anxieties and reflect on his decision to empty out the bag rather than just explaining my mistake.

Dominic's car was the first to be returned. It had had a hard three years traveling Europe from East to West and North to South, through the tulip fields of Holland where the landscape stretched for miles and was 90% sky, to the snow capped mountains of the Alps where the sky was claimed by rocky outcrops and mountain passes. It had been filled with souvenirs, African chairs, packed lunches for long journeys and small boys dropping scraps into the gaps and a dog slobbering into the crevices.

The car was to be passed on to another family beginning their adventures and we felt we had a duty to remove our memories and grime to allow room for theirs. We arranged for it to be professionally cleaned and when we picked it up it looked like new. We parked it in a multi-story car park next to Dominic's work and drove away from our "adventure chariot" reminiscing of all the vistas it had transported us to.

The next day Dominic left so that he would be in Boston to greet Matilda and we prepared for her to leave the following day. She had arrived in Germany at only a year old, not fully grown, in the biggest crate that any company made. After a few schnitzels and a pretzel or two, she had continued to grow and now was too big for the crate so a new one had to be custom made. Of course, since it was made by Germans it was the most beautiful piece of engineering that you could imagine with a water bowl and tube from the outside to fill it. We expected that the next day this palace for her to travel in would arrive and she would be ready to fly across the ocean to the land of big steaks and wonderful fish, but we were disappointed as we discovered she needed to remain in Germany for one last evening of love at the local pub. The weather was too hot in Boston for her to fly so she was delayed by 24 hours. We took her to the Fasel Stalle for one last evening in the beer garden. They loved her in our town. When we had said we were leaving the barmaid looked like she was about to burst into tears. I was touched that they felt we were such an important part of the community that we would be missed, but my illusion was shattered when she announced, "No Matilda auch?"

Eventually, the temperatures in Boston fell and the next day Matilda was loaded into a big van in her crate for her luxury flight to Boston. A little while later the boys and I were picked up for our flight to Iceland and our trip home. Iceland was one of the places on my bucket list, along with Japan, New Zealand and Rome, and this was our chance to tick off a land of mystery and fables.

Landing in Iceland felt like landing on the moon. It was such a barren landscape with black grey rocks everywhere. The taxi driver that took us from the airport to our apartment, pointed out the Blue Lagoon as the plumes of smoke rising from behind a rocky outcrop and I explained to the boys that we would be visiting there as part of our tour of the Golden Circle. Later when we were in the amazing lunar landscape with the warm bright blue waters apparently making us healthier by the minute, I overheard two separate sets of Americans making disparaging remarks at people drinking wine at 11 am in the hot springs and three separate lots of Brits saying how great it was there was a swim-up bar! This kind of summed up the main thing that we had learnt over the last three years. However, similar we think we all are, our different cultures make us see the same situation in a totally different light. A couple of years later with the arrival of Trump and Brexit, this was to change from fascination at the differences to a disappointment in the inability to embrace others differing views. This, in turn, would lead to the realisation that although we were glad to have the chance to experience Europe, it was to become much more difficult for my children to do the same when they reached the world of work.

When we got to our apartment we soon discovered that you could never escape volcanic activity in Iceland. All of the heating and hot water was geothermal and the shower doused you in water that stunk of rotten eggs. The next day, we headed down the only main street that seemed to make up Reykjavik and at the top of which our apartment was situated. Only a few yards down the road was a sign for a museum and we hurried to look through the window to see if it was worth a visit. The whole window was filled with giant penises and statues of animals, mythical creatures and men, all with the common feature of an enormous appendage. The boys' eyes lit up as they started to head inside, but I told them it was probably not a museum we would be visiting today, as my American puritanism started to reemerge! We headed towards the coast popping into shops to try and find souvenirs and a Christmas tree decoration to add to our collection from every country we had visited.

Soon we found a Viking museum which seemed much more appropriate and, after learning all there was to know about the first inhabitants of this fabulous island, we had worked up quite an appetite. We had already examined the menus of all the restaurants we had passed and, as we had been warned, discovered Iceland was very, very expensive. Therefore, we decided to plump for fish and chips from a van outside the museum. Surely that would be a nice cheap option. Oh no! It really wasn't! For four tiny portions of fish and chips, we paid sixty Euros which seemed very overpriced. After a trip inside a glacier, another to geysers, waterfalls and the Blue Lagoon and Henry being very proud that Iceland had allowed him to stand in one continent and pee into another, we set off back to Boston and the life of a refugee in a Marriott Residence Inn.

Here we were all squashed into three tiny rooms with a giant dog, our suitcases and boxes of "essential items" ranging from a large apple wine jug to a wide array of scrapbooks, photos and mementos. Within a week or so we were called into school to discuss Henry's progress and draw up his IEP. His teacher informed us that she really thought that we should have him tested for ADHD, as he could forget things and at times did not hang his coat up or get his supplies out of his bag as quickly as she would like. Her goal in testing, although she did not say it directly, was to medicate him into compliance. The woman who had, most likely, never moved beyond the neighbouring town and thought that going abroad was venturing into Maine or New Hampshire, was completely clueless as to what it was like for a boy, who had only just had his 8th birthday, to move to a new country of which he had no memory. This new country had totally different expectations and language and be expected to suddenly, and in fact immediately, learn a whole new set of routines whilst living in a hotel room which was constantly being rearranged by the daily cleaning staff. In one lesson she had asked the children to tell her another way to say quarter to three. Henry's hand flew up eager to answer.
"Viertel vor drei!" he shouted proudly when she called on him. He was used to being asked to say things in a different way be it German, British English, or American English, positively trilingual!
"No Henry. Anyone else? Yes, that's right 2.45!"
Henry had no idea why his answer was wrong, indeed probably because it wasn't! When his homework was returned covered in red crosses because he had answered similar questions in similar ways, again he had no idea why his teacher was angry with him. Then when his homework asked him to explain why 45 minutes was 3/4 of an hour and he asked me for help. I asked him what he thought and he said, "Well when Mrs. Minute has walked 3/4 of

the way around the clock she has got to the 9 and 9x5 is 45 so she has taken 45 steps,"

I told him that was a great answer and to just write that down, but he said, "My teacher doesn't have a good imagination and she really isn't very adventurous, so I need to write it the way she will understand."

He knew that she was a linear thinker, devoid of any concept different to that which had been instilled into her uncompromising brain 30 years earlier, but that he wasn't that kind of thinker and that needed to alter his thinking to make it easier for her to understand. He has a mind, and indeed a life, that leaps from one adventure to another requiring instant reconfigurations, but she had a life in which one day was indistinguishable from all the others and in which no alteration was necessary. She liked it that way, however, and wanted no surprises in her student's homework and no opportunities to see things from a different perspective. He ended up writing 9x5 is 45 and nine is three-quarters of twelve, which seemed so sad, but acceptable. He learnt in those first few weeks that creativity and uniqueness were not tolerated in the American system and he needed to adapt to conform.

James had been the victim of similar narrow mindedness several years earlier when his 4th-grade teacher had told him that she had "no intention of listening to such a ridiculous accent" for the whole year. She had made the whole class point at the immigrant (James). On the whole, America saw us as the right kind of immigrant, but occasionally you got to experience what it was like to be the wrong kind of immigrant. In Germany, I felt more often that I was the wrong kind of immigrant, told to go to the back of the line because it was, "Deutsche zuerst" or berated in-front of a shop full of ice cream consumers because I did not pronounce "Erdbeere" correctly. You understand what it is like to fight to make your way through a country where you are always battling to understand and be understood. You know that learning a language takes years not months even with intensive instruction.

On September 2nd the tenants had moved out and I had the first day with my own washing machine since the second week in July. I found this sadly exciting! However, the lack of understanding from others about children traversing cultures and the joy of my newfound ability to wash clothes seemed insignificant when our container finally arrived (although we were glad that it had not been left in a lay-by somewhere between Hamburg and Frankfurt in retaliation for us allowing the German driver to do nothing!) Anyway, the guys at the American end were not much better, although in fairness it was just the guy who lead the team that caused us problems. He was super grumpy and even when I heard a massive crash in the back of his van he insisted that it was nothing to do with him and nothing was broken, even though the box in his hand was all bashed and full of tiny bits of crystal glass that looked like the result of a huge diamond heist. Even Matilda didn't like him and we had to keep her locked up for fear that her aggressive bark escalated. When we checked off the boxes from the first container somethings were missing, but he insisted that we sign to say they were all there. I was a seasoned traveller by now, so I obviously refused and he became very aggressive and a little scary. I told him to leave as I would not be intimidated, my face stern and steadfast, but my heart pounding and stomach churning. After a lot of emails and phone calls and an English, "Das geht nicht!" to a man used to passive aggression not blunt reality, the offending gentleman was replaced by a nice man called Joe. who even Matilda approved of.

When everything was unpacked we decided to share a little bit of Germany with all our friends by having a German Party. We asked everyone to come dressed as their favourite German and served German beer and sausage. I was Maria von Trapp and Dominic Herr Captain Ludvig von Trapp, and we welcomed people carrying towels under their arms to reserve a chair in the best German tradition. Anna and Paul came with German flags on their heads tied with chords like a strange nativity play, soft toy lambs under their arms, two German Shepherds of course! Henry was a German beer, James, Martin Luther and Edward Angela Merkel, although I have never seen Angela Merkel sat with her legs wide open, dress bunched up around her waist, underwear on view, playing X box. It all seemed a long way away from the life we had just left and I realised our adventure was over.

Just as we thought our memories of Germany would fade into the distance an email arrived from Germany with a photograph of the beautiful spotless car we had left in the car park, eagerly waiting for a new family it could transport to faraway lands and new discoveries. The car had sat in the carpark for three or four months as the new family packed up and prepared for their move. The keys had now been handed over to the father who had rushed to the parking lot in search of a shiny new vehicle to take home to his family, allowing them to make the mandatory trip to Ikea and the supermarket, the government offices and the bank, possibly to buy beds so they did not have to sleep on a hard floor lined with blankets or even save their dog from last-minute extermination!

The memories of our family should have been erased from the Black BMW, but as he approached, the tendrils of its previous occupants filled every inch of its interior. Our attempts to wipe clean our existence and present him with a new start had failed. The car had been placed back in the parking lot immediately after cleaning. The fresh smell of pine and mountain air was the evaporation of the water which was supposed to have washed away any traces of our family, but as the car was sealed and left for three months these traces could not escape. The mould spores which emanated from dropped food and dog dander could not escape either and in the perfect now damp surroundings they thrived to produce webs of white, green and yellow mould which stretched from one side to the other obscuring any view of the luxury interior. Even hot steam and cleaning products could not erase us from the German psyche and nothing would erase our memories of our time there.

As James and I started at the British school, me as a special ed teacher and him as a GCSE student everything seemed mundane. The car in Germany was recleaned and the new family's adventures began in the repetitive cycle of unique ex-pat relocation experiences, that mirrored all previous experiences. I started Orton Gillingham training and rushing from place to place, panicking I would never get it all done and the days of strolling through the fields on a sunny evening to the Fasel Stalle faded into the mundane monotony of everyday life.

21 A LESSON LEARNT

You only regret the things you don't do, was my motivation for moving to Germany. I returned with no regrets, but no real ah-ha moment. That came a couple of years later as I wandered along the white paths that skirted the hallowed halls of the Melaka mosque, in a backwater of Malaysia. I was a superstar in a hijab. Here I felt that I belonged, a Christian in a muslin place of worship, blond hair peeking out of the blue fabric which surrounded my porcelain skin, surrounded by the warm glow of smiles emanating from dark-skinned faces that squeezed in for a selfie with this alien caucasian. I could not help but think of how I felt more alien surrounded by the fake smiles of the ex-pats, who had travelled to Germany in search of adventure, determined to enlighten the locals with news of PTAs, trick or treating, and hotdogs like missionaries bringing measles to the Amazon. These families refused to visit Turkey or Morocco missing out on the vibrant colour and wondrous aromas of spices in the markets and the warm smiles emanating from hijab lined faces because they feared a Muslim uprising.

Here I was in the centre of a Muslim uprising. An uprising of love and acceptance. They had no wish to change us, but instead were enchanted by our differences and wanted to share the wonders of their own culture, pointing out beautiful hidden gems around the mosque that may have gone unnoticed. The tiny ladies huddled around Edward encouraging him to stand even taller, so that his red hair thrust into the blue sky far beyond his 6ft 5 frame. They bent their knees slightly emphasising the height difference, giggling as they snapped selfies with the strange giant that had appeared from nowhere. These were not my people, but now for a moment, they were. We had more in common than I had with the expats coffee moms who worshipped my god and shared my colouring.

What decides the crate or basket in which you belong? Before I left Lancashire I believed that I was defined by my birthplace and by the birthplace of my ancestors, but these giggling Far East beauties were not from my place. My place was no more than a dot on a map on a schoolroom wall to them.

I knew belonging was not related to birthplace after a year or two in America. On trips home, as I utilised new vernacular and challenged perceived wisdoms, like the correct side of the road on which to drive, I was no longer one of them, but had evolved into the one who had rejected them. I had taken on strange ideas, believing young people should be valued rather than demonised, accepting the gap in every American bathroom stall that stole your privacy for no apparent reason and having tea in a to-go cup in my car. Some places back home though were still my crate. With my friend Julie, with whom I had grown from a naive eleven year old, battling teenage spots and supporting each other through failed adolescent crushes, I had a sense of acceptance and belonging. She had married the acceptable northern lad, had an acceptable highly successful career as an accountant and settled down in the acceptable town of her birth and had not wandered from the preordained path. We may have followed different paths, but yet we had the same worries, the same frustrations and the same joys.

Laurie, also from the Midwest, but far removed from the Midwest coffee moms, had shown me it was not a shared place of birth. Michelle and Julie, firmly rooted in the soil of their birth place, had shown me it was not the shared experience of travel that brought with it kinship, but it took time to process what it was that I needed to belong.

It was the trip to the mosque that allowed me to piece it all together. Those who made me feel the sense of belonging were not linear thinkers. All were out of the box, critical thinkers with an acceptance of other philosophies that differed from their own. Julie would live vicariously through my adventures, as I did through her comfort with the familiar. Laurie threw herself wholeheartedly into anything on offer, accepting the hilarity of failure and the joy of newfound pleasures. Michelle opened her home and her family without question to anyone in need of a place to sigh deeply into a comfortable chair, as she soaked up ideas ready to share her wisdom sympathetically when needed. The ladies in the mosque were drawn to the differences, whereas the expat coffee moms were drawn to creating uniformity, their uniformity.

As a tide of political change seemed to be enveloping the world like a deathly tsunami of intolerance, I saw this fear of differences breeding pain and disquiet. I wished that those who had not yet seen the joy in diversity could be enlightened, as I had been through my experiences in Germany where I had learnt what was most important in life. My ah-ha moment took a year or two to shape itself, but I eventually discovered it is more important to be at peace than to be right, a skill that I am still struggling to perfect, but know is worth pursuing. I discovered that you need to accept others may have their own, equally beautiful, "right" and that that may be different from my "right". Most of all, I became determined to fill my basket only with those who have that same goal: refusing to put their own ego before contentment! If like-souls were unavailable, I learnt to become content with my own company.

Luckily this journey to wisdom allowed me to fill my celebration fruit basket with a couple of newly found odd fruits who each earned a place there because they saw the beauty in every fruit that they nestled between in my basket.

ABOUT THE AUTHOR

Katherine Gostick was born in 1970, in a sleepy rural village in Lancashire England, a place she believed she would never leave. Somehow, however, she ended up living in America and Germany observing the quirky differences as she navigated the different cultures with her husband, Dominic, three young sons, James, Edward and Henry and huge Newfoundland dog called Matilda. She used humour to survive and realised that even if you fail you will still have a good story to tell, so you may as well give things a go.

Printed in Great Britain
by Amazon